PENGUIN B(

ROADWALKER

Dilip D'Souza was educated in Pilani, Providence, Delhi, Rishi Valley, Mumbai, Cambridge, Austin and places in between. Once a computer scientist, he now writes for his supper: about political and social issues, travel, sports and mathematics. Computer science stresses clear thinking, reason, logic and getting to the heart of the matter. Maybe those things shape his writing. Maybe not.

His writing has won him several awards, including the Statesman Rural Reporting Award, the Outlook/Picador Non-Fiction Prize and the Newsweek/Daily Beast South Asia Commentary Prize. This is his ninth book.

Dilip lives in Mumbai with his wife Vibha, children Sahir and Surabhi, and cat Aziz. He misses his Rhodesian Ridgeback, Shaka.

PENGUIN BOOKS

ROAD WALKER

A FEW MILES ON THE **BHARAT JODO YATRA**

DILIP D'SOUZA

PENGUIN BOOKS

An imprint of Penguin Random House

PENGUIN BOOKS

USA | Canada | UK | Ireland | Australia
New Zealand | India | South Africa | China | Singapore

Penguin Books is part of the Penguin Random House group of companies
whose addresses can be found at global.penguinrandomhouse.com

Published by Penguin Random House India Pvt. Ltd
4th Floor, Capital Tower 1, MG Road,
Gurugram 122 002, Haryana, India

Penguin
Random House
India

First published in Penguin Books by Penguin Random House India 2024

ISBN 9780143463412

For sale in the Indian Subcontinent only

Typeset in Goudy Old Style by MAP Systems, Bengaluru, India
Printed at Replika Press Pvt. Ltd, India

www.penguin.co.in

MIX
Paper from
responsible sources
FSC
www.fsc.org   FSC® C016779

To you who walked

Thank you:

Joy Ma, Stefanie Borkum, Nikhil Lakshman, Ramani Atkuri, Ghazala Wahab, Mukulika Banerjee, Rajshree Chandra, Rajmohan Gandhi, Yashasvi Vachhani, Pervin Varma, Sahir: who read.

Karthik Venkatesh: who pushed me.

Vibha, Surabhi, Neela: the spring in my steps.

But above all: Those on the Yatra whom I walked with and spoke to, who helped me, who kept me going, who gave me spirit and hope. Too many to list, but you all know who you are. Let's do it again!

Contents

Introduction

A Day (or a Few) on the Yatra

It's a cold January night in Ambala, Haryana. I'm sitting on my bed in a friend's house, working out arrangements for the next morning and the one after. This involves looking up a website, matching what it says against the day-wise schedules someone has sent me and then locating places and global positioning system (GPS) coordinates on a map. This is followed by a series of calls to hotels and taxi drivers. This takes far longer than I would like it to, especially because my friend is waiting for me with an aromatic home-cooked dinner.

When I'm finally done, the arrangements look something like this: a taxi will pick me up at 5.30 a.m. tomorrow. The driver, someone with the intriguing name 'Rimpy', will drive me more than 50 km to the town of Sirhind in Punjab. After dropping me there, he'll drive on for another 25 km to the town of Khanna and leave my small backpack with most of my clothes at a hotel there. I have persuaded the man who answered the phone at the hotel to keep the backpack for me until I arrive.

For arrive there I will—sometime tomorrow evening. I'll collect my backpack and spend the night. The next day, another taxi—no intriguing name for the driver— will pick me up at 4.30 a.m. and drive me about 20 km to Doraha. Dropping me there, he'll drive on another

22 km to Ludhiana with my small backpack. Not to a hotel. He will wait for me somewhere near Samrala Chowk in the centre of the city. I will get there sometime that afternoon. Given the crowds I suspect I'll be in the middle of, I'm just slightly anxious about meeting him easily. But once I do, he will drive me to the Ludhiana bus station. From there, I will take a bus to Chandigarh. It will get me there too late for a flight home, so I will spend the night in another hotel.

Day three: back home.

If all that sounds complicated, it seemed just the same when I was planning it and working out the details. But over the next two days, it all worked like a dream. Rimpy was there on time, chatty as he drove. He made no complaints as various road closures meant we had to take a long detour to get to the spot in Sirhind

I had to reach. He delivered the backpack to the hotel, which turned out to be a slightly strange—try bright red and black sheets and a geyser in an external ventilation duct—but serviceable establishment. The second driver actually spent the night—an even colder night—in his Maruti Eeco outside the hotel, to be sure he'd be there for me in the morning. He was chatty as we drove too.

That afternoon, he was waiting as close to Samrala Chowk as he could get, which was still a couple of kilometres away. Indeed, with the massive crowds and traffic restrictions, we had some trouble locating each other. But he turned up, with my backpack and a son in the passenger seat. Instead of waiting most of the day for me, he had actually driven back to Khanna for a shower and a change and brought his son along on the drive back. 'He's preparing for his twelfth-standard exams,' he told me. 'Please give him some advice.'

So, as we drove to the bus station, I said a few things about finding out what he really liked doing, about working hard but also taking the time to relax and get his mind off the exams. I keep the faith that it helped.

Worn out, I slept all the way to Chandigarh. At the hotel, I slept some more before hobbling to a nearby restaurant for a tasteless dinner. Hobbling, because it had been that kind of day. Days. With the adrenaline drained, the flight the next day was almost an anticlimax.

All this, in service of my urge to join the five-month-long caravan—bandwagon? cavalcade? what?—known as the Bharat Jodo Yatra. Rahul Gandhi and his Congress Party kicked it off in Kanyakumari on 7 September 2022; it would conclude in Srinagar at the end of January 2023. Here, in Ambala, I was joining it for the third time.

* * *

The logistics were a tough nut to crack, but necessary. The *yatris* themselves—those walking the entire route—had barely enough accommodation for themselves, none really for pop-ups like me.

So why was I popping up in this fashion anyway? Why wasn't I walking the entire route?

Before the Yatra began, I never once considered joining it full-time. I'm not sure why. It certainly wasn't that I doubted my physical ability to do it. I walk a lot, I play tennis, I swim, my at-rest pulse is usually about 56 . . . of course, months of daily 25–30-km treks is a daunting challenge, but somewhere inside me, I knew I could handle it.

So was it a mental block that kept me from joining? Did I not take the idea of the Yatra seriously? Maybe I didn't know how to become part of it, meaning whom to ask and what to do. Or perhaps I simply assumed I had too many other everyday preoccupations to even contemplate taking several months off to walk the length of India.

The length of India, though. Think of that. The magnitude of it takes my breath away, even months later. When next will I get such an opportunity? As the Yatra got going, through its early days in Tamil Nadu and Kerala, that question began to haunt me. Through those early days, the challenge of finding an answer came to mean something to me. Something deep, profound, elemental. The challenge of the walk, yes. But what it helped me articulate for myself, too. The way it dredged up long-ago experiences, reminded me of what they had meant, wrung new meaning from them now, said things about my country, my family, myself. All in all, it helped me decide—if I wasn't doing the whole trip, there was a next best thing I could do.

So what was that next best thing? Simple: join the Yatra for a short stretch. By the time the idea took shape and began to demand fruition in my mind, the Yatra was already a couple of weeks old. It had wound its way through Tamil Nadu, was nearly finished with Kerala and would enter Karnataka soon. Videos were circulating—curious crowds along the route, policemen almost jogging to keep up with the pace, Rahul Gandhi taking part in a boat race. Each was compelling enough on its own; together, they tugged at my heart, my senses, my mind, in ways I had not thought possible.

I had to join the Yatra.

* * *

When I finished that long planning session on my Ambala bed, it was well past midnight. I had only a few hours left for sleep before Rimpy would arrive. I worried a little about walking all day on so little sleep. But outweighing the worry was the anticipation, an almost feverish tingling in my bones. Walking was still a few hours away, but I could actually feel the adrenaline kicking in already. That told me I'd be fine tomorrow.

4.30 a.m. I'm awake and still tingling, shivering but not just on account of the cold. After a quick shower, I can barely get my limbs through my clothes. My friend produces a small, shiny, silver-coloured bag. 'There are raisins and nuts in here,' she says. 'Eat them as you walk.' I stuff the bag in the pocket of my jeans, and somehow that's when I open a gaping tear in the worn fabric of the jeans, just above my left knee. Can't be helped though.

I have two or three shirts, but only that pair of jeans. Tear or not, it will have to do.

Rimpy has a flowing grey beard and, even so early in the morning, chatters non-stop. He drives at a steady 90 kmph, but even so, most of the traffic so early in the morning shoots past us. Nearing Sirhind, we pass a gaggle of tents lit up by bright lights: the camp for the yatris, where they all must have spent the night. *No need for them to work out intricate logistics*, I find myself thinking, feeling mildly annoyed and mildly sorry for myself, momentarily forgetting about the infinitely larger operation the Yatra is, requiring far more intricate logistics.

Just past the camp, by my map only a couple of kilometres short of where the Yatra will start today, we come to a dead halt. The road ahead is blocked by a few police vehicles, lights flashing. Some cops are waving their arms to our right, indicating that's the direction we should go. We have no choice, so Rimpy makes the turn and barrels down a narrow country road. Google Maps shows us a left turn ahead that will take us where we want to go. But when we get there, there's a bridge or something like it under construction and no way to turn left. On we go, and I start despairing of reaching the start point.

But there's Rimpy. '*Koi gal nahin!*' [No problem!] he says twice as we drive, that familiar Punjabi phrase calculated to ease any worries. At some point he suddenly turns left, then right, then takes a U-turn under some kind of bridge, then we're going the wrong way on a service road below a long flyover, then he U-turns on to the flyover and it makes a wide curve to the right and then descends to another cop waving his arms, by which time I'm totally lost even with my Google Map staring up at me from my phone. '*Koi gal nahin!*' says Rimpy again, because by some miracle, we're here. For beyond the cop, I can see a huge crowd. I alight, and before I can say a proper goodbye, Rimpy and my little backpack have U-turned and disappeared.

Beyond the crowd, there is a stage. It's early morning, and cold, and the people on the stage, presumably politicians, are making loud speeches. The Congress hand is everywhere, as are plenty of bunting and flags. And the people! Everywhere I turn there are more. Milling around, sitting on the ground, listening to the speech-making, not listening to the speech-making. This being Punjab, the majority are Sikhs, wearing turbans in a cornucopia of colours. One, in a particularly handsome purple one, comes up and says, by way of introduction, 'O.P. Jindal!' I should have been fast thinking enough to say 'BITS Pilani!'

but I settle for a baffled look. He explains that he is a student at O.P. Jindal University and has come from there to join the Yatra. Before I can ask, or even wonder, why he chose to tell me this, and especially with that opening, he is gone, a friend dragging him closer to the stage.

On a small traffic island, two men stand in front of a life-size poster of Rahul Gandhi doing a namaste. One wears a deep-blue *bunga* (tower) style of turban that Nihang Sikhs favour, his robes the same deep blue and what looks like a sword in a bright red scabbard protruding from below his pure white jacket. With his grey beard and folded arms, he is the picture of gravitas, but both men smile slightly when I ask if I can photograph them. I'm still proud of the resulting image—it's almost as if Rahul Gandhi is greeting them. Elsewhere, there's a tap on my shoulder and I hear my name. It's my friend Shakil Ahmed from Bombay, now walking with the Yatra. I had

met him while with the Yatra in Rajasthan a few weeks ago.
It's astonishing that, in this huge gathering, we've bumped
into each other again.

It's the crowd awaiting the start of today's walk,
of course. There are little groups everywhere, chatting,
laughing, high-fiving. Some sit on the ground, some
on the flatbeds of parked trucks, some on the steps
of shopfronts shuttered this early morning, but most
stand. I'm not sure how many are actually listening to
the speeches—I certainly am not—but everyone seems in
a uniformly good mood. Most of the talk is in Punjabi—
not my language, but I had plenty of Punjabi friends in
college. Thanks to them, I understand snatches around
me, particularly the ones that have the words 'Rahul
Gandhi', or 'Congress', or 'Yatra'. Those, the same
whether in Punjabi, Hindi or English. There is an energy

among them, an anticipation, almost an electricity, that I pick up on gradually, but surely.

It takes a while, but I finally figure out where the road out of this spot is, which people will take when the Yatra actually begins this morning. Not easy, because there are at least four possibilities that I can see, and nobody I ask knows which one it will be. The giveaway, finally, is the barricade that I see a few cops almost unobtrusively stretching across one of the roads.

The act of blocking that one is itself a sign, and it's not just me who notices. Within seconds, the crowd gravitates to the blockades. I'm lucky in that I was close to the cops when I noticed what they did, but the press of the crowd, pushing me against the barricades, is quickly unsettling. Shakil is to my right. Somewhere behind me, some slogan-shouting starts up.

We are, yes, still awaiting the start of today's walk. I am still paying no attention to the speeches on the stage to my left and behind, as those around me aren't as well. I have no idea whether Rahul Gandhi is speaking or has spoken or will speak, but I surmise that once he finishes on stage, he and his entourage will move off-stage and then via some route that I cannot see, to the road in front of us. The police want to keep the road relatively empty, so all that can happen smoothly. Once they are there and moving, the barricades will open, all of us will flood through and start walking.

But the wait for that moment is unsettling. The crowd is now restless, heaving, seeming just moments from pushing against the barricades; the sweating, nervous, too-few cops on the other side pushing back, shouting at us to wait, to stay calm. These snatches of Punjabi, I understand in full. But nobody is particularly calm. I have visions of stampedes, of tripping and falling and being trampled when the blockade is lifted. It feels very real. Shakil gives me a wan smile. He must feel it too.

There's suddenly movement on the road ahead, though I swear I didn't see anyone, let alone a Gandhi and an entourage, making an entrance from the left. The crowd starts shouting. At some signal I don't catch, the cops pull the barricades—well, one!—aside and scurry to either side. Scurry they must, or they will be overrun. For too many of us are squeezing through that too-small opening. I focus on simply keeping my balance, putting one foot deliberately in front of the other, and that serves to get me safely through the opening. Most of the flood breaks into a run, intent on catching up with whatever's ahead. Shakil is not the sort to run, but I've already lost sight of him. I'm content to walk, conscious I'm behind much of the Yatra, aware that I would like to overtake much of the Yatra, but I have at least the rest of the morning to do so, for now simply glad I haven't been trampled.

And just like that, the caravan gets moving. It's 11 January 2023, Day #117 of the Yatra.

1

Unease: Despair of the Past Several Years

On Day #117 as on the other days I joined the Yatra, a question came up repeatedly. People would ask me—it was a good icebreaker every time I met someone on the Yatra for the first time—and it would also resonate in my mind.

In its simplest form, it looked like this: Why was I walking? It took more convoluted forms too. What was driving me? What were my concerns, apprehensions, expectations? What had led me here? And more broadly, was there common ground with the others walking? Did they have the same concerns and expectations, or similar ones? What was the Yatra going to do to address those?

At some level, I promised myself I would answer these questions fully only later, after the Yatra was over. That was because I had a feeling the Yatra would help me articulate an answer better than I could on my own. But at another level, the answers kept coming, taking shape, as I walked. In that, I felt a definite solidarity with the others walking with me. For whatever reason, the Yatra fostered a certain clarity of thought. For me, that took me back many years, through many incidents and emotions, perhaps all the way to a moment on the terrace of my parents' block of flats in Bombay.

It's not often that I delve into prehistory to explain present-day motivations and doings, but here I think a dose of that did me some good and gave me that clarity when I needed it. Let me explain what happened on that terrace and let me relive one more episode.

* * *

In some ways, my political awakening was the Emergency of 1975–77. I was fifteen when it started and in my last year of school in Delhi. It was the first time I remember being at all aware, and reacting to, the political realities around me. When I joined college in Rajasthan (BITS Pilani, like I mentioned earlier) in 1976, we incoming students took an exam to determine our level of written English. For the essay that was part of the exam, I wrote a screed against Indira Gandhi and her Emergency. The result? I was exempted from first-year English courses. The essay did that for me, though I later got a quiet caution from one of the professors who had graded the papers. 'Be careful about what you write publicly like that,' he said. 'You're lucky it wasn't passed on.'

He didn't specify to whom it might have been passed on.

Still, I was just a teenager, and most political ideas in my head then were nebulous and yet to be shaped in any real way. That's why I think of that moment on the terrace. Sixteen years later, that was my real political awakening.

March 1992. I had been away from Bombay, the city I grew up in, the city I called home, for over seventeen years by then: more than half my life. We left at the end of my Class X for New Delhi, where my father had been transferred. I did my last year of school there—the old Class XI Indian School Certificate exam—and then went to Pilani for five years, pursuing a degree in engineering. Done with that, I left for Providence in the USA to pursue another degree, this one in computer science. Done with that two years later, I found a job in Texas and moved there. Nearly nine happy years later, I made the decision to move back home to Bombay.

Looking back on those years, one remarkable aspect was how out of touch with India I was. Those were the days before ubiquitous internet access—I had it at university in the US and at my jobs, and it was spreading quickly through those years, but really only in the US and Europe. There was no Twitter or something similar to feed us news in real time, like we have today, and newspapers and television in the US rarely covered

Indian news. My only source of regular Indian news was via regular letters from home, in which my parents and friends often sent clippings from Indian newspapers. That's how I learned, for example, of a tense strike at my Rajasthan alma mater in 1983, and India's cricket World Cup success that same year.

But I entirely missed the Indian films and cricket matches of those years, and—pertinently—had only a hazy idea of the political goings-on in the country in that time. Mrs Gandhi's assassination and the slaughter in Delhi in 1984 made headlines in the US, certainly. They would. But not the Khalistan movement, nor the Bofors scandal, nor the Mandal agitation, nor the rising temper of the Babri Masjid–Ram Janmabhoomi dispute, nor the growing questions about the idea of 'development' asked by such organizations as the Narmada Bachao Andolan. These and more were themes I heard snatches about from the clippings in the post, or from speaking to friends who returned from India, or from my own brief trips home in 1985, 1988 and 1990. But stuck in the USA as I was, there was no easy way to find out more. It wasn't that I knew nothing about those currents in India. It was instead as if I had just dabbled in them, dilettante-fashion, without being steeped in them as I might have been if India were really my home. And the more the years went by, the more I did want to be steeped in them, because I could sense the way they were shaping India. Shaping my home.

The result was that I returned to India in early 1992. The result also was that I very quickly started learning things about my country I had only dim ideas of. Awakenings aplenty.

Everything around me was new, but like a rediscovered old sock: so familiar and yet a little distant. It wasn't the

India I had left behind in 1981. Plenty had changed.
But it wasn't an utterly transformed country either, as
it would be over the next few decades. In those first few
weeks back, I revelled in it all. I wandered all over my
city to rediscover it. Took a long train ride to a remote
corner of Madhya Pradesh to see my brother and his wife
at the rural hospital where they worked. Interviewed with
a software company in Andheri, who made me a good
offer, but the work simply didn't excite me.

And that March evening, I strolled up the stairs to my
parents' terrace with my camera. The setting sun, the sea,
plenty of crows and the occasional kite: I had a good time
shooting it all.

Until three men barged through the door and
accosted me. 'Who are you?' 'What are you doing?' 'Where
are you from?' 'What's that?' (pointing at my camera.)
They barked the questions at me faster than I could

reply. They weren't happy when I did answer, mentioning my name, that I lived in the building, that I was taking photographs of the evening scene and that it was, well, a camera. And while I had a good idea who the men were, or at least what their profession was, I thought one barked demand for my identity deserved at least a polite request for theirs. Which polite request I made.

By way of response, one of the men produced a gun and pointed it at me, its muzzle no more than an inch from my forehead. I invite you to imagine what it is like to look into the barrel of a revolver that's that close. I invite you to imagine what it is like to think of a bullet erupting from that nozzle when it's that close. It's hard. Or more correctly, it's nerve-shattering.

The men then grabbed me, one by the belt loop at the back of my jeans, and began shoving me down the stairs, intent on taking me around the corner from the building, to the office of the Assistant Commissioner of Police (ACP). Luckily, we ran into my initially bewildered and then outraged parents emerging from our front door, two flights below. Luckily, the men knew my father, or at least of him, because of his long career in the Indian Administrative Service (IAS) and the respect he had earned. So they left me there and disappeared down the stairs.

The next day, a senior from the ACP's office brought the cop who had nearly shot me, to give us an 'apology'. I wasn't particularly interested in one anyway, but he undermined any sincerity I might have sensed when he said: 'I did not pull out my gun.' Apparently, my memory of that nozzle was pure fantasy.

But as upsetting as this incident was, the real reason I remember it is not so much the gun, not the bald-faced lie about it, not the finger yanking up my belt loop, none of that.

A few months later, the late playwright Vijay Tendulkar filed a petition in the Bombay High Court, asking for a panel to monitor police high-handedness. He cited several incidents to support his case, including mine. In response, the police filed an affidavit 'on behalf' of the then Police Commissioner of the city. And somewhere in those typed pages, in black-and-white legalese, lay a political awakening.

For according to this affidavit on behalf of the Police Commissioner, when the policemen 'questioned' me that evening, I told them my name was 'Shaikh'.

Understand, I did nothing of the sort; I told them my actual name that you will find on the cover of this book. Understand too, and again, it isn't this bald-faced lie either. The affidavit asserted that when they heard this name—they didn't—the 'extremely watchful' policemen on the terrace became suspicious. 'There was no explanation given . . . by the said Dilip D'Souza as to why he had falsely stated his name as "Shaikh".' (Aside: my memory of that gun must really have been a fantasy. The affidavit also stated: 'It is absolutely false that the police officers concerned pointed a gun at the said Dilip D'Souza.')

The implications have stayed with me. Why hadn't the Police Commissioner's affidavit chosen 'Taneja' or 'Murugan' as the name I had 'falsely stated' that day? Why a Muslim name? Because whoever drafted it wanted, even expected, the High Court to believe that a Muslim name was self-evidently reason for suspicion. Because they assumed that if they used 'Murugan' instead, the High Court would be unlikely to believe this concoction.

Think of it. What if my name was indeed 'Shaikh' anyway? Is it inconceivable that I could have been doing just what I was doing, photographing the sunset and the crows? Or what if my name was indeed 'Murugan'? Would the cops have promptly put away their guns and trooped off the terrace?

Recalling that affidavit often reminds me of Colin Powell, the American general and politician. When Barack Obama was running for President in 2008, Powell distanced himself from his own Republican Party and publicly endorsed Obama. By way of explanation, he said:

I'm also troubled by — not what Senator McCain says — but what members of the [Republican] party say, and it is permitted to be said. Such things as, 'Well, you know that Mr. Obama is a Muslim.' Well, the correct answer is, he is not a Muslim, he's a Christian. He's always been a Christian. But the really right answer is: 'What if he is?' Is there something wrong with being a Muslim in this country? The answer's no, that's not America. Is there something wrong with some 7-year-old Muslim American kid believing that he or she could be president? Yet I have heard senior members of my own party drop the suggestion, 'He's a Muslim and he might be associated with terrorists.' This is not the way we should be doing it in America.[1]

Again: My name is not 'Shaikh', nor did I ever claim it was. But that's almost irrelevant. The really right response to that poisonous affidavit is to ask, 'Well,

---

[1] Alana Wise, 'In 2008, some Republicans claimed Obama was a Muslim. Colin Powell pushed back', *NPR*, October 19, 2021, https://www.npr.org/2021/10/19/1047127311/colin-powell-barack-obama-muslim (accessed October 2, 2023).

what if his name was "Shaikh"?' Why should that make cops suspicious?

Instead of acknowledging a relatively simple mistake, the policemen on my terrace, with their superiors, chose to fabricate a story. They used the Muslim name because they thought it would bring immediate credibility. What did that say about the police, the judiciary, the idea of justice, society at large? Us?

Over the following months and years, I have often found myself wondering: just what would have happened had that lout of a cop pulled his trigger and spilled my brains on to my terrace? Would I have been just another victim of a police 'encounter'? Just one more in a lengthening list that has people who should know better applauding? How many in that list are, like I might have been, shot dead and then labelled the 'notorious gangster

Shaikh'? After all, it would be a case of my word against the cops', except that I'd be dead.

All of which is arguably why that was the moment I first started to ask questions about the climate, the politics, in my country.

The answers? Disturbing.

As a less serious aside, some of all this also obliquely explains why I refer to my city as 'Bombay'. I have no objection to 'Mumbai'; in fact, I like the sound of that name. All of us who live here have always called it 'Bombay' while speaking English, 'Bambai' in Hindi and 'Mumbai' in Marathi. Much like 'London' and 'Londres', or 'Germany' and 'Deutschland'. So I never quite understood the compulsion to insist on 'Mumbai'.

But that apart. Political goings-on in those early '90s resulted in a Shiv Sena–Bharatiya Janata Party (BJP) coalition government taking office in Maharashtra in

1995. One of their early endeavours was to officially change the name of the city to Mumbai. In 1996, they held a celebration to mark one year in office. Among other things celebrated was the change of the city's name.

The city remained just as strewn with garbage, commuting conditions for its millions remained just as strenuous and difficult, justice for the murderous carnage of a few years previous remained just as elusive. But hey— the name was now officially 'Mumbai'.

That was the moment I thought to myself, *I'm going to call it 'Bombay' just as long as I want.*

* * *

In the mid-1990s, my wife and I were invited to a gathering of 'inter-community' couples—in which wife and husband were from different communities. By 'inter-community',

I had assumed the organizers meant marriages across religious lines. Now at the best of times, religion does nothing for me. Thus my cynicism: I expected to hear an entire evening's worth of platitudes that would go in one ear and out the other, and then we'd go home.

But what was fascinating that evening was the sheer gamut of couples that thought of themselves as 'inter-community'. Start with a Chitrapur Saraswat married to a Goud Saraswat: two strains of Brahmins, both Hindu, both of whom call Konkani their mother tongue. But to them, and to others in the two communities, there are profound differences. No wonder they believed their marriage was an unusual occurrence—because it bridged those differences.

That's why they were there, that evening. In turn, my marriage into the Chitrapur Saraswat community is the reason my wife and I were there. Like the others, we were

expected to say a few words about what the differences
were between us and why we chose to look past them.

All evening, 'adjust' was a word we heard a lot.
'We had to adjust quickly!' 'His mother is the one who
had to adjust to me!' Food and language, these were
two major themes that needed the pair to adjust. That
applied even to the two Saraswat strains. But Konkani is
their language, you say. And how vastly different could
their cuisines really be? Well, the Goan Konkani of the
Gouds is substantially different from the Mangalorean
Konkani of the Chitrapurs. And Gouds like their
daily diet of fish, which isn't exactly the usual fare on
Chitrapur menus. So adjust they must, and did, and
seemed blissful about it.

Later, a Hindu woman walked on stage, her Catholic
husband behind her. In their case, the barrier they had
crossed was between religions. More than food and

language, that's what they spoke of: they had a church wedding, they had a temple wedding, both families initially opposed their marriage, but over time the opposition melted away. People nodded their heads—this spectre of familial opposition was clearly a familiar one— and clapped.

Towards the end, we heard from an Indo-French couple, then an Indo-Armenian one. Their stories were again different: how much the foreigners, despite some early hesitation, had come to like India, Indian ways and Indian food; how lovely their Indian wedding ceremonies had been; the way the Indian spouses had reacted to foreign cultures; the challenges of bringing up children in such a home.

Were these broader divides than the one between Chitrapur and Goud Saraswats, and does the word 'broader' even apply here? Only if we on the outside wanted to see them that way. For as we moved along, the lesson slowly sank in: 'community', 'adjust', 'divide'—these words were only as narrow or as broad as any of these couples chose it to be. From how they spoke, the amount of adjusting, the effort, the challenges, actually seemed—well—broadly similar. Take me: I never saw much of a divide between my wife and me, and I think I can speak for her too.

Though the organizers did have in mind some kind of ordering of divides. The Saraswat pair early on, with others like them. The Hindu-Catholic pair in the middle, with Hindu-Muslim and other such, including language 'divides', packed around them. The multinational types at the end. Somewhere in that spectrum, my wife and I. From differences within a particular sub-caste, we moved smoothly along to differences between religions, and thence, still smoothly, to differences between nationalities.

In short, each couple was being celebrated that evening for what we had done. Celebrated, amazingly, for doing what had come only naturally to us. The organizers wanted to recognize that, even if none of us thought about it much, our marriages were unusual, significant, maybe even profound. The idea of the gathering, then, was to celebrate our contributions, by simply getting married, to building an India we might all cherish. And that's how it went. As each couple came up on stage and spoke a few words about their particular experience, the organizers gave us each sweets and a small memento and the audience applauded warmly. It was easy to take home the thought—because we the couples in that room had crossed our various lines, India was a better place.

That was 1996. Looking back from this India of 2023, it seems almost naïve, almost sepia-toned, almost ancient history. I read about the nonsense of love jihad, and I marvel at how much a country has changed. I wonder: *who would even think today of such a gathering, such a celebration?*

Take what happened to Tina Dabi and Athar Amir-ul-Shafi, IAS officers of different religions whose marriage in 2018 caused conniptions in some circles. Today, I wonder where in that evening's parade they would have been positioned. I'm especially curious because they got a remarkable amount of abuse for doing what came only naturally to them. This remark, for example—only typical, really—was directed at them on Twitter: '*Dabi. Rajputo ka surname hai. Shadi miya bhai se. Dub maro Tina. Ma baap ka naam roshan kiya hai. Rajputo mai ise miye se jyada good looking hai. Jai Mata di.'* ['Dabi' is a Rajput surname. She has married a Muslim. Drown yourself, Tina. You have done your parents proud. There are better looking Rajputs than this Muslim. Victory to the mother(land)][2].

That's right. This man wants Tina Dabi to drown.

And all these years after 1996, the Government of Maharashtra announces a panel[3] that will 'gather information about inter-caste and inter-faith marriages'.

---

[2]   This was the link for the tweet: https://twitter.com/ss_r1206/status/983499852947513344 but it has since been deleted.

[3]   Aupama Katakam, 'Maharashtra forms committee to track inter-caste, inter-faith marriages', *Frontline*, December 14, 2022, https://frontline.thehindu.com/news/maharashtra-forms-committee-to-track-inter-caste-inter-faith-marriages/article66263241.ece (accessed October 2, 2023).

That's me and my marriage. I've never even thought of us as 'interfaith', and yet here it is, a panel readying to 'gather information' about us because it thinks we are interfaith.

In fact, within just a few months, apparently this panel has received plenty of 'complaints'. What these complaints are about, I don't know. But the panel will 'investigate' them. And I think, what if one of those complaints is about my wife and me? What gives anyone, above all a government panel, the right to 'investigate' our marriage? Or anyone else's, for that matter? And what if they find, or concoct, some black mark against my wife and me? What will they do to us then?

All just more questions to ask, of course. Here's where we have come: from celebrating marriages between communities to officially investigating them. Take that as a measure of the climate, the politics, in my country.

* * *

There's so much more. Absurd lies about the Muslim population overtaking the Hindus, matched only by ludicrous lies about the Christian population doing the same. (I've lost count by now of how many times I've written articles mathematically debunking this nonsense.) The go-to response to critics: 'Go to Pakistan!' The spate of lynchings of Muslims, followed invariably by investigations and arrests of the (surviving) Muslims themselves (what kind of meat was in that refrigerator, Mr Dead Muslim?). The garlanding and celebration of lynchers. The carnage in my city in 1992–93, followed by the carnage in Gujarat in 2002, followed by endless inquiry commissions whose proceedings are routinely delayed or stalled altogether; whose eventual findings are either anodyne or ignored, so that pretty much nobody is ever punished for those horrific crimes. And if they are, the wheels of the justice system churn so that they are released and feted on their release. The ever-more open threats against Muslims. The insidious rewriting of school textbooks to remove not just the Muslim pages in our history, but to remove any remotely critical references to Hindu extremism. The day that, no matter what many say, will live in infamy: 6 December 1992, when a mob tore down the Babri Masjid. The snarling hatred and scorn for me on the faces of men I met in Delol village in Gujarat in early March 2002—men whom, I came away convinced, must only days before have murdered many of their neighbours. The friends who must have nursed nauseating prejudices all through our friendship, because now they feel no compunctions spouting them. The wellsprings of anger in too many around me—at perceived injustices to their particular communities, perceived kid-glove treatment of other particular communities, specific politicians.

I could go on. And on.

Hatred, bluster, bigotry, anger, illogic—it's all part of our national canvas today. I'm fully awake now, politically, and there are times I wish I wasn't. I wish I was back in the more innocent, less suspicious, less frightened, more caring, more empathetic India I grew up in.

But of course I'm here. This is me, this is now. And in this here and now that too often gets me down, there came the Bharat Jodo Yatra.

2

Indecision: To Walk or Not to Walk

There came the Yatra all right, but it wasn't immediately clear whether I should, or would, join it.

At one level, this was a familiar feeling. About many important things in my life, I've had a hard time deciding what to do. Weigh the pros and cons, of course. I don't know how that goes for others, but for me, and too often, neither pro nor con wins decisively.

So about me and the Yatra, The Clash had it right when they sang their hit, 'Should I Stay or Should I Go?' Should I go on the Yatra, because there are people to meet, places to see, experiences to be had, views to listen to and learn from? Or should I stay, because there are dentist appointments, books to read, friends to meet, articles to write? Should I stay, because there's comfort in taking the easy option? Or should I go, because there's excitement and a challenge to face down?

The French have a word for the back-and-forth that goes on in my mind. They call it *tergiversing*. Well, they probably do not use the '-ing' suffix. But it always takes me a while to get over it, and it was the same with the Yatra. In the end, what tipped the scales was that I knew I would forever regret missing the chance. The Yatra may or may not make history, and that's okay either way. But this was my chance to make my own slice of personal history, entirely for myself. That was enough for me.

Having decided that, there were plenty of logistics issues. How do I reach the constantly moving target the Yatra presents? How would I actually join? How would I leave and find my way home? Could I stay with the yatris; and if not, where would I stay? What were the arrangements for food, for toilets, for water? How much should I travel with, and should I assume that I would have to carry it all on my back as I walked?

Lots to work out. But once I decided to go, all this became secondary, almost trivial. In fact, I found I didn't really care what the answers to those questions were, just that there would be answers.

And that those answers would help me find answers to some much more profound, soul-searching questions that were welling up in my mind.

3

Rationale: Why I Walked

Several years ago, the country was captivated by Dhanush's song '*Why This Kolaveri, Di?*' [Why this murderous rage, girl?]. Its relatively catchy tune, the comical lyrics, the obvious fun the singer and his friends were having in the recording studio—all made for an unlikely but memorable hit. On YouTube, the video has racked up well over 400 million views. It also gave us an almost existential question that you could ask about anything at all. Life, work, significant others, tragedy, farce, politics, cricket . . . 'Why this kolaveri di?' somehow managed to speak for musing and wonder and angst in any of those directions, and it did not even need an answer.

In the second half of 2022, I caught myself occasionally humming the same tune, but with a different lyric: 'Why this Bharat Jodo Yatra?' With the extra syllable, the timing was off. But that didn't matter—after all, I was the only listener. But after a point, it wasn't just a light-hearted reference to an amusing song. It started taking on the same existential quality the original did. It started speaking for the same musing and angst, in all those same directions. Again, there were no real answers necessary. In simply asking myself that rhetorical question, the Yatra started taking on meaning for me. Not because Rahul Gandhi and other members of the Congress were walking it. But because, in an originally nebulous way that grew slowly clearer, the Yatra became a focal point for me. It became a vessel into which I believed I could drop all the themes about my country that I have agonized over for years. Not drop and forget, but drop and stir and watch, for maybe this would produce answers that have so far eluded me.

I don't expect that to happen immediately, and later I learned that plenty of the others I met on the Yatra felt the same. But there was a value to the simple feeling of solidarity, to knowing that others felt similar angsts.

Consider some examples. Three thousand of my fellow Indians were slaughtered in Delhi in 1984, after the assassination of Indira Gandhi, solely because they were Sikh. To me, this has always been the worst crime, the worst act of terrorism on Indian soil ever. Clearly though, not everyone agrees. Because nobody of any consequence—make that nobody—has been punished for that horrific carnage. Innumerable inquiry commissions did what they had to, what they were designed to—offer the illusion of justice, turn our attention away. But what happened to Congress leaders H.K.L. Bhagat and Sajjan Kumar, for example, whom many witnesses say they saw leading the murderous mobs?[4] Kumar was sentenced to life in prison in 2018, a

---

[4]   Witnesses said this to the Justice Nanavati Commission of Inquiry into the 1984 massacre. For example: from its Report, page 160: 'Shri Kishandev Singh has also stated that he had seen Shri Sajjan Kumar in the mob, which had attacked his house.' Page 166:

full thirty-four years later. Bhagat died in 2005 without facing a modicum of justice for what he was accused of.

A generation later, what do we tell Sikhs who lost family members then? Or Sikhs who were born afterwards but who grew up hearing about the massacre? With what face do we ask them to believe in India?

Eight years later, over a thousand of my fellow Indians were slaughtered in Bombay, after the demolition of the Babri Masjid. And on 25 January 1993, Justice B.N. Srikrishna was appointed to conduct an inquiry into the violence over the previous several weeks. This

---

'Ms. Kamlesh has stated that on 31-10-84 she had seen Shri Bhagat addressing a crowd of persons and inciting it to kill Sikhs and as a result thereof on the next day her house and other houses in the locality were attacked by a riotous mob.' Full report available here: https://www.mha.gov.in/sites/default/files/2022-08/Nanavati-I_eng_3%5B1%5D.pdf (accessed 5 October 2023).

was an expected step. Setting up an inquiry commission is standard operating procedure for governments faced with public outrage over violence, such as communal riots. This is because this particular kind of violence invariably has three significant features: first, that the government law and order machinery fails in its duty to protect citizens; second, that this machinery frequently participates in rioting itself and third, that the rioting is instigated, cheered and led by powerful politicians the government is reluctant to punish.

All three features were part of the slaughter in New Delhi in 1984. All three were features of the violence in Bombay in 1992–93.

I sat through much of Justice Srikrishna's deliberation and was left appalled, shaken to my core. At one point, I felt compelled to walk up to a man who had just testified, one Madhukar Sarpotdar of the Shiv Sena, and tell him

that I was ashamed he was my Member of Parliament
(MP). (He wasn't happy. 'Meet me outside!' he screamed.)
But it wasn't just the antics of many like him, people
who only wanted delay and obfuscation. It was also that I
learned a lot about how inquiry commissions are treated,
and that was especially dismaying.

By now, governments know that inquiry commissions
are the ideal sop to offer to people demanding punishment
of criminals in massacres like we saw in Bombay in
1992–93. For inquiries come with several outstanding
features themselves. First, they take a long time to be
completed and second, they can be delayed even further
by innumerable frivolous adjournments and other time-
wasting tactics. But if these two can be called operational
shortfalls, perhaps, three other features come directly
from the way the Commissions of Inquiry Act, 1952 is
treated, judicially speaking.

Any Commission set up under that Act 'shall have the powers of a Civil Court', it says, in certain matters such as summoning and examining people, receiving evidence, asking for documents and so on. Also, what takes place before a Commission 'shall be deemed to be a judicial proceeding'.

Yet a Supreme Court judgment from 1977[5] is only one such that spells out what this language in the Act really means, judicially speaking. (It actually refers to an even earlier judgment, from the Nagpur High Court in 1954.) The judges observed that 'the Act merely clothes the Commission with certain powers of a civil court but does not confer on it the status of a court . . . the Commission is only fictionally a civil court'. What's more, 'there is no

---

5 *State of Karnataka vs Union of India and Another*, https:// indiankanoon.org/doc/184521/ (accessed October 2, 2023.)

accuser, no accused and no specific charges for trial before the Commission, nor is the Government, under the law, required to pronounce one way or the other on the findings of the Commission'. In short, a Commission is just 'a fact finding body meant only to instruct the mind of the Government without producing any document of a judicial nature'.

Thus: the government is not required to make the report of the inquiry public; an inquiry is a fact-finding body, not a court of law and therefore has no powers to punish people that it finds have committed crimes; and in any case, the recommendations of an inquiry commission are not binding on the government.

Justice Srikrishna wrote a remarkable report after his inquiry was complete. There was no equivocation; he named names, he made several recommendations, he reminded us of all we had experienced and knew in those terrible weeks. Are you surprised that there's been no action taken as a result?

There's plenty more to say about this, about happenings in the last thirty or so years. I won't spell all that out here. But the reason I mention the massacres of 1984 and 1992-93 is that they capture, like really nothing else does, my continuing angst about my country. I am a tax-paying citizen of this country. Do I have the right to expect justice? And if the answer is no—as the fallout of these episodes resoundingly suggest—what is going to happen to my country?

So let me repeat my questions from a few paragraphs above. What do we tell my fellow citizens of Bombay who lost family members in 1992-93? With what face do we ask them, or anyone, to believe in India? And yet this is not just about Sikhs, or the residents of Bombay. What do we tell anyone in this country who wonders about justice, democracy, the rule of law, themes such as those? What do any of those words mean when not only do these massacres happen in our largest cities— one of them our capital—but we care nothing to punish the guilty?

* * *

At some level, such questions have knocked around inside my brain for years. It has been hard to believe, and accept, that what seemed to me these simple notions— mete out justice, punish the guilty—are actually hotly and forever contested. Where you stand on them depends on, of all things, your political leanings. The slaughter in Bombay, for example: I've heard innumerable people refer to it as the city being 'protected'. Meaning, a certain political leader and party stood up to 'protect' us all from the possible depredations of . . . whom?

Plenty unsaid there, and again, I'll leave it that way. The point is really my almost impotent anger, my voiceless anguish, over all this. I never know whether to be encouraged or depressed that, over the years, I have found many more like me—filled with the same emotions, yet unable to find a way to express them in a way that might make a difference.

Me, I've written innumerable columns on these and similar themes. Arguably at least five of my eight prior books touch on them too, to some degree or another. By and large they—columns and books—have been received well. I get the occasional pat on the back from a reader here, a student there, even a politician or two. Yeah, it feels good. But it feels inadequate. I'm acutely conscious that

I write in English. That therefore I reach a small slice of India. That even if some small slice of that small slice takes home from my writing something to think about, there's a huge ocean of humanity out there I've never reached and probably never will. How do I get over this hump, then? Not that I expect to reach everyone in that ocean, but is there a way to at least feel like I'm part of something bigger, something that might make a difference?

At the risk of belabouring the point, that something appeared in 2022: the Bharat Jodo Yatra.

One politician, his party, their journey on foot across the length of India. At any other time, this might have filled me with cynicism. In fact, that's not a 'might'. When I first heard of this Yatra, I certainly was cynical. After all, I remember the last such, from over thirty years ago. I was contemptuous of and disgusted by L.K. Advani's 'Ram Rath Yatra' of 1990, because it seemed to me that Advani plotted it only to stir up hatred for political benefit.

Was this one going to be much the same?

The first sign that it would be different: whereas Advani rode in a Toyota dressed up as a chariot—any irony lost on him and his faithful—this politician actually walked. Notwithstanding my feeling, shared by many others, that he would start off walking but eventually jump into a nearby vehicle, or even give up on the Yatra altogether—notwithstanding that, he kept walking. And walking. And so did many others with him. Day after day after week that turned into months. By about the second week of the Yatra, as I watched this caravan wind through deep southern Tamil Nadu and into Kerala, as I marvelled at the ever-larger crowds and their enthusiasm, the cynicism began to melt. This man and his party were going to keep this up, all the way to Kashmir.

And I had to join. I had to walk too.

I mean, through those early weeks, it wasn't just that the cynicism disappeared. The certainty grew too, that in some form I couldn't quite articulate yet, I belonged there, walking. Something about it reached out all the way to my soul.

It took me a while to fully comprehend why that was. Here, finally, was something being done to address my own angst. Not explicitly like that, of course. Not necessarily guaranteed to be successful, of course. But somehow that didn't matter. For at least the Yatra seemed to be born of, guided by and suffused in themes such as justice, a voice for the voiceless, democracy, love, empathy and secularism in its true sense. In being so, it spoke for me. Because these are the ideas and values that I grew up with in this country, that I therefore took as givens. Yet they are the ideas and values that I have watched being crushed over the last several years. So much so that it's gone beyond despair; I had started to wonder if it was I who had the givens all wrong. If justice is so easily subverted and ignored, was it really the given I had assumed it was? If it is so easy to hate, to drum up hate, does it actually become slightly embarrassing to speak of love instead? If my name alone marks me as someone whose loyalties to India are suspect, can I ever expect to be treated for who I am—simply Indian, simply human?

Not meaning to drive the point into the ground, it's not just that these were and are my concerns about my country. Judging from everything I heard and saw on the Yatra, they were and are the concerns of plenty of my fellow Indians as well. Which is why they walked.

* * *

One day on the Karnataka leg of the Yatra, my little group sat down with a group we had been walking with all that morning. This was in the afternoon break between the two sessions of walking. We were sitting in chairs outside two enormous tents. One had dozens of cots on which the yatris were resting. The other had long tables at which people sat to eat a simple lunch, served to them on bright green banana leaves.

Finished with lunch, our new friends were discussing why they had joined the Yatra. Mohan, a squat man with a greying beard, seemed to be working through his reasons right there and then, musing in some wonder: 'You know, I've been anti-Congress all my life. So why am I here at all?' He stopped to collect his thoughts. 'It's just that now there's this assault on Indian democracy,' he said. Several people nodded. Nobody needed Mohan to spell out what he meant. He went on: 'So I want to defeat that and save democracy.'

He seemed suddenly aware of the full weight of what he had just said. Then: 'It's much better that we start getting organized a year-and-a-half before the elections, instead of only a month before.' Several others nodded again.

Soon after, Mohan got up to leave. After two days with the Yatra, he and his friends were returning home that afternoon. It was only after he disappeared that I realized I had not actually said bye. For I had been sitting there, lost in thoughts spurred by his words.

Yes, the Yatra was happening a year-and-a-half before the 2024 Lok Sabha elections. Yes, it was a largely Congress show. Yes, Rahul Gandhi dominated the coverage. Yes, there were and are questions about the Yatra's purpose and meaning, even among the small group I had come with. But with all that, there was still an overriding focus among many who joined the Yatra: never mind past disagreements, never mind the need to hold your nose if you have to. For now, there's a shared imperative: stand up and be counted, against the party in power today.

Seen that way, it's an ironic reminder of an earlier moment in our history. That's when a group of parties came together—looking past disagreements and holding their noses, yes indeed—to form a coalition to jointly fight the upcoming election. I refer to 1977, of course. Ironic, because the shared imperative was to stand up to the party then in power—which was the Congress. And that year, the motley Janata coalition managed to dislodge the Congress. That the coalition didn't last is another story, but in 1977 their great success was defeating the Congress.

During and after the Yatra, I was not persuaded that it would—or even could—build up momentum and strength on that 1977 scale. But in some ways, and at least for now, that was irrelevant.

One face of the Yatra was the Congress. You might say, and you'd be right, that it's a party in some disarray and depression, because of its nosediving political fortunes over the last several years. It has lost elections, it has lost veteran Congress-wallahs, it has factions sniping at each other. If this Yatra was a way to rebuild political capital, to galvanize Congress activists, to show the Indian voter that this party will not roll over and fade away—well, for anyone who values Indian democracy, that's welcome.

But another face altogether of the Yatra—and that's the face that truly caught my attention and imagination—was the diversity of people who joined. There were people like Yogendra Yadav, or Mohan above—known and severe critics of the Congress in the past. But there were others as well, and they came to the Yatra with their own incredibly varied palette of issues. I mean LGBTQ activists and farmers, manual scavengers and schoolkids, unemployed youth and nomadic tribes and many more. Again, if the Yatra was a vehicle for them to bring their concerns to the attention of the Congress, but also to the country as a whole—well, that was welcome too. Because to me, this rich, colourful diversity is the authenticity and promise of India itself. It's what breathed spirit and life into the Yatra.

And why was I there? Partly, of course, because the Yatra set my journalistic antennae to quivering sharply.

I wanted to simply watch and observe, in some sense not even really invested in the success or otherwise of the Yatra. But mostly, as I spelled out above, this was something I felt I had to do to stand up to the divisiveness, the hatreds, the polarizations that are marking out and deepening so many fault lines in this country. My solidarity with—luxuriating in, more like it—the diversity of India may mean very little in any broader sense to anyone else. But it meant a great deal to me, and that's what took me to the Yatra.

But there in Karnataka, I was also accompanying a small group of public health professionals. Two of them were Ravi and Ramani, my brother and his wife, doctors trained in community health. They have worked in primary health care for years in rural Odisha, Madhya Pradesh, Chhattisgarh, Rajasthan and Gujarat. Two other friends and colleagues, Guru and Prasanna, were along as well—not doctors, but they have worked for years with public health outreach organizations.

Over several days before we joined the Yatra, the four of them had prepared a brief on public health concerns—malnutrition, right to health care and more. Their goal was to hand the brief over to the Congress leaders in the Yatra, including Rahul Gandhi. (They gave it to me to read and I had a couple of minor suggestions, which is why they added my name to the brief.) Through various contacts, we had actually scheduled a meeting—during the midday break on the Monday we walked—with Gandhi and others. Our group would present the brief then. Only, that meeting was cancelled the evening before. There were a few too many groups lined up during that midday break; some farmers, particularly, wanted to meet Gandhi. So instead, the organizers arranged for us to walk with Gandhi for a while that morning.

Once we were positioned alongside him and walking, Ramani and Prasanna spoke to Gandhi about the brief. Now I'm terminally cynical about politicians, and especially at a moment like this when Gandhi was surrounded by surging crowds calling his name and wanting photos. It's a measure of my cynicism that I honestly did not expect him to really pay attention to us. But even while waving out every now and then and acknowledging the crowd, he listened closely to the brief. He asked a series of questions, challenging and making Ramani and Prasanna back up their data and conclusions.

One example: Ramani mentioned her experience with migrant workers in Rajasthan. They get injured at work and try to get the free health care that is available in that state. But because their Aadhaar card is from Bihar, say, they are denied treatment. Why should that be? But Gandhi asked, well, how will a state cope if floods of people from another state come in to take advantage of the announced free care?

After a while, I took the chance to speak to Gandhi about my book, *The Deoliwallahs: The True Story of the 1962 Chinese-Indian Internment.* I said that while I admired and respected his great-grandfather, this imprisonment of 3000 Chinese-Indians was one of his mistakes. My co-author Joy Ma, I pointed out, was born in the camp and spent her first four years there. The Chinese-Indian community is longing for an acknowledgement of and apology for this injustice. Gandhi listened carefully, then asked me to send him a copy of the book. Which, a few months later, I did.

We remarked how well the Yatra was proceeding. Gandhi said that was true, but we should remember that organization and mobilization are two different things.

What we could see on the Yatra was mobilization. That's easily done, but it is short-lived. What the Congress needs, he said, was to transform mobilization into organization. In Kerala, he said, the party can organize and so it is effective; in other places, it is much less able to do the same.

Guru suggested he attempt an east–west Yatra too. Gandhi laughed and asked: 'Will you join me then? All 3000 km?' Guru laughed in turn and said he would.

Just as we were moving off to the side to leave the cordon around Gandhi, he turned to Ravi and said: 'Hey, I didn't hear from you. Is there something you want to tell me?' So Ravi spoke. He urged that if and when the Congress returns to power, it should pay attention to health care. In particular, it should ensure health care is not completely privatized, because that will take it out of reach of the great majority of poor Indians.

For sure, all of us were grateful for the chance to raise our concerns with Rahul Gandhi. But that was just the icing, really. It was the full experience of our days with the Yatra that really left us stimulated and encouraged. That repeated on my subsequent stints as well.

In what is otherwise a time of hate and darkness, the Yatra lit, in the words of a friend, 'a tiny glimmer of hope in our hearts'. Good reason to be there. Still conscious that I might be driving the point into the ground, it's why I went.

4

Fellow Travellers: Others Who Walked, with Me and Otherwise

Asceptical friend asked: '*Bharat jodne ka kya plan hai Congress ke paas?*' [What plan does the Congress have to heal India?]

Not a bad question to ask before I joined the Yatra, but, as I realized, especially after. Because it had me musing, reflecting, reminiscing—and then I tried to answer it.

My first time on the Yatra was, as I mentioned earlier, with a small group in Karnataka. We got a taste of its spirit even before we started walking. Early one morning, we stationed ourselves 2 km ahead of the walkers' starting point. The GPS coordinates had been sent to me by WhatsApp—the digital age, after all. Ahead, because someone had told us the best place to walk was just in front of the main body of yatris: still among plenty of walkers but not engulfed in a flood of them jostling for space on the road. So we waited there for the Yatra to arrive. I strolled about, taking photos of nearby posters and bunting.

Out of the blue, someone on a truck yelled as I passed: '*Majjige!*' I showed incomprehension, so he said, helpfully: 'Buttermilk!' and thrust a small green packet at me. He was unloading several sacks filled with the same packets, all for the walkers, and must have decided I needed one.

Nearby stood a stall selling coconut water. Out of the blue again, a police van stopped, several men in plain clothes leaped out and asked the stall-owner for coconuts for all of them. With a large machete, he began slicing one. Suddenly perturbed, the cops grabbed the machete and examined it closely: what if the vendor had nefarious intent? But persuaded somehow that he wouldn't use the machete to leap into the Yatra and start hacking at humans, they handed it back and he continued slicing the coconuts.

Things got more serious quickly. We were engulfed in a tide anyway, jostling for space on the road. Those pictures of Rahul Gandhi, walking briskly with hardly anyone or anything ahead of him? That's achieved by a police cordon around him and stretching for a good 50 metres in front—an actual long rope carried by dozens of cops. They walk on the edge of the tarred surface.

To keep the cordon intact, they summarily push nobodies like me out of the way. So I fell in among plenty more like me, and then further behind because I had no stomach for jostling.

Yet here's the thing. Not one person I met complained about the jostling. Nor about the hours of walking, not strolling. Nothing. I mean, I had my reasons for walking. But what were some of the other walkers thinking?

Take Chandy from Kerala. He was one of the 150-plus yatris, men and women who did the whole journey from Kanyakumari to Kashmir. The first time I met him, he and two women walking with him did a jig right there on the road, laughing in delight. Then I kept bumping into him—sometimes he caught up with me, sometimes I caught up with him, once or twice we walked side by side for a spell. If he didn't do the jig again, he was in the same good spirits every time. But get this: he was barefoot. Every time. Yes, he did the whole trek—several thousand kilometres—barefoot. After meeting him, I couldn't help thinking of him every now and then when I wasn't on the Yatra—this cheery man, trekking along on his bare feet.

'How's the walking this morning?' I asked him on Monday when I came up from behind and he was hobbling slightly. It had rained overnight, and Chandy said, 'All fine, except the rain has woken up all the grains of granite. So instead of lying down sensibly, they are poking upwards into my feet.' And on he hobbled. I walked ahead to catch up with a companion. An hour later, Chandy overtook us.

Take Meghana from Bengaluru. She came alongside once when I was just ahead of the cordon, walking behind the press truck. In an almost booming tone, she demanded to know: 'So what brings you here?' My reply was almost meek in comparison to her apparent sternness, but I soon realized it was just her way of speaking. In the same booming tone, she told me she had worked as a gynaecologist for many years, but then gave it up and joined politics. Specifically, the Congress. Then when this Yatra was announced, she knew: 'I had to join. I had to walk. This country needs this now.' I wanted her to flesh that thought out, but was preempted by another booming demand: 'Have you come alone?' I shook my head and pointed to my sister-in-law Ramani, striding along a few feet away. 'She's a doctor too,' I said. Meghana promptly lost interest in me, moving over to shake hands with Ramani: 'Hello, I'm a doctor too,' I heard her say, and then they moved steadily ahead, chatting animatedly about whatever doctors chat about while on a Bharat Jodo Yatra.

Take Ankit from Delhi. A Congress worker, he had been assigned a specific task: stride in front of the Yatra, walkie-talkie in hand, barking out instructions to sundry vehicles to preempt accidents and smoothen the yatra's progress. At one point he noticed the two slow-moving press trucks getting a little too close for comfort. I know because I was walking between them at the time, just starting to wonder if I was going to be squeezed. 'What's going on?' he shouted, practically in my ear, but actually at the two drivers. 'You both want to kiss each other?' (It sounded far juicier in the original Hindi, not least because of his barking.) Seeing several of us break into smiles, he turned to me and said: 'See, I'm going to walk like this every day till Kashmir. It gets boring if I don't find ways to make it fun!'

Then something ahead of us caught his eye. 'Hey, Fortuner!' he yelled. 'Yes, you fat Toyota Fortuner! Move up ahead, at once!' (Oh yes, it sounded far funnier in the original Hindi.)

* * *

There were others. Plenty of others.

One morning in Karnataka, I caught up with a tall man who had a slight limp. We greeted each other, then I tried Hindi first, for a conversation. He said a few words in response, but it was clear he didn't really know the language well. 'English?' I asked. A little better, he said. Then he tried me: 'Malayalam?' I shook my head no, and tried some Tamil, my mother tongue, even though my Tamil friends snicker. He smiled broadly. And with my less-than-fluent Tamil and his halting English, we chatted happily as we walked.

Follow the yellow! Musicians in Karnataka

Clearing up after the Yatra, Karnataka

Virender Singh greets the children, Rajasthan

The eyes and the smile say it, Rajasthan

Follow the yellow! Yatris in Punjab

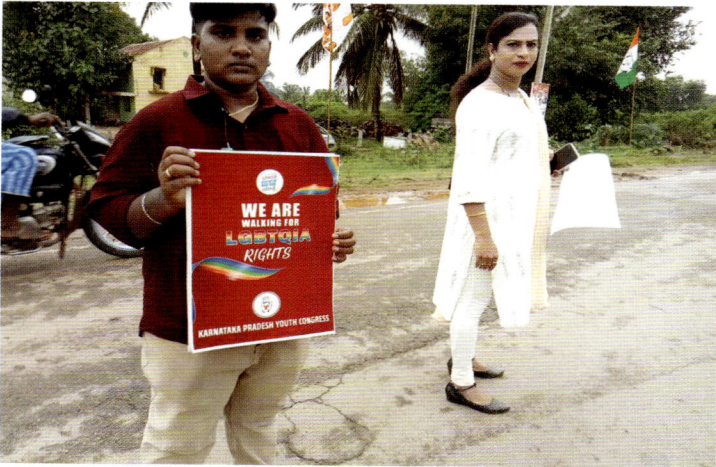

Pride on the march, Karnataka

Lal Chowk emotions, Kashmir

Chandy does his barefoot thing, Karnataka

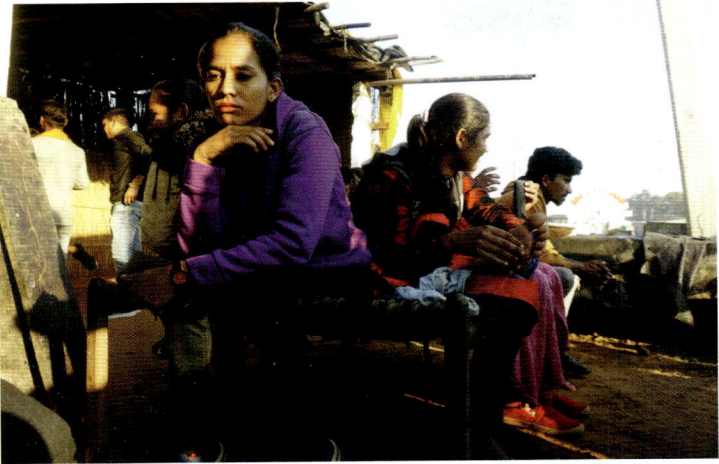

Chai break on low charpoys, Rajasthan

Chairs abandoned, Rajasthan

Coconuts for all, Karnataka

Dancing on the march, Karnataka

The Tiranga in the mist, Punjab

The band hits the road, Punjab

Holding back the hordes, Punjab

Walking with the Yatra, Rajasthan

He was a doctor from Kozhikode. He had joined the Yatra in Kerala, intending to walk only for a couple of days. But a couple of weeks later, here he was in Karnataka, still walking. His plan was to return home when the Yatra left Karnataka.

And why had he joined anyway? He had three English words in response: 'Too much hatred.'

* * *

At some point while walking, as I've noted before, I had worked out that the best place to position myself was right behind the media vans and trucks. They were several dozen metres ahead of Rahul Gandhi, that expanse kept essentially empty. They were piled high with photographers and other journalists, and a man who operated a drone somewhere above us, staring intently at the video feed. The vans moved at a steady walking pace. I kept up easily, though I couldn't help wondering what it must feel like to drive these vans in first and second gear, at that steady walking pace, for several months.

Sitting on a tiny empty space on the edge of the bed of one of the trucks was a young woman in a rust-coloured sari, chatting amiably with the reporters. Every now and then she'd step off, walk for a while, sit back again, repeat. It was my first day on the Yatra, and if I was to judge from her easy camaraderie with everyone around her, she was a veteran.

After a tea break, I found her walking now, to my left. For the time being we were just ahead of the press vans, and for the time being she wasn't retiring to her spot on the truck-bed. Walking alongside her was a boy, about eleven or twelve years old. I offered him a candy from my pocket, which broke the ice. He gave me a wide smile, she asked for a sweet too. She was a lawyer in Bengaluru, taking a break from her practice to walk with the Yatra. 'There are others in the office who will manage while I'm away,' she said. 'This is important.'

To my surprise, she said she had arrived only the previous morning. 'But it looked like those press-wallahs were your good friends!' I remarked. 'No, no!' she said. 'I met them just yesterday.'

She was heading back to Bengaluru that evening. Pointing to the boy, I asked, 'And what about your son, is he off from school?' 'No, no!' she said again. 'He's not my son! I don't even know him! He was standing on the side of the road this morning, and he just started walking with me.' Just like that, this kid had walked several hours with her. When she peeled off to return to Bengaluru, he would too, to return on his own to his home, several hours behind us.

I gave him another candy. He smiled again.

* * *

At a morning tea stop on the highway to Ludhiana, all of us sank gratefully on to whatever flat surface we could find. It had been a longer stretch of walking than usual, and I certainly welcomed the break. My chosen flat surface was actually an empty cart—the kind that fruit or vegetable sellers use.

Sitting there sipping a cup of hot chai, I saw a few of my walking chums off to my right, chatting up a young boy outside a shop. To my left, another yatri was talking to a group of women, residents of a nearby home for the disabled. Just the usual at these stops, when impromptu conversations with curious onlookers would invariably start up.

Suddenly, there was a tap on my shoulder, and I turned to find Jahnavi standing there, smiling. We had met on my previous Yatra stint, in Rajasthan, and walked together for a short while. Three weeks later, here I was on the Yatra again, and she came over to say hello. 'What happened to you, all these weeks?' she wanted to know.

I explained that I could not be with the Yatra for long stretches. 'But here I am now!' I said. 'And you?' I asked. 'You've been walking since we last met?' She nodded. We chatted for a short while again. Like the man from Kozhikode, she was—in her own words—'just deeply disturbed by the hatreds'. That's what brought her to Maharashtra, well before Rajasthan, where she fell in with the Yatra. 'When will I get a chance again,' she asked, 'to be part of something like this?' A question I remember asking myself, as it happened.

After a few more moments of pleasantries, she crushed her paper cup, threw it into a nearby bin and set off. She liked walking a few minutes ahead of the bulk of the Yatra, she had told me. I'd catch sight of her like that— later that day and the next, and again in Kashmir, some weeks later—50 metres or so in front, her hair bobbing as she walked. Once, though, I found her sitting on a bench outside a petrol pump. 'Twisted my ankle slightly, so just resting! I'll be okay,' she said. Indeed. Not long after, I caught sight of her again, 50 metres or so in front again. No, I don't know how she overtook me. Nor when.

The last time we met, it was a freezing Srinagar early morning. With three other yatris I had run into, and because there was no other transport available, I was walking to where the Yatra was to start that morning, on the outskirts of the city. We stopped for a quick chai and some biscuits. Several soldiers were there, also partaking. Jahnavi walked in a few minutes later, with a man I remembered from among the yatris I had met. Bundled up in a heavy yellow jacket, she was still visibly shivering, until the chai came. 'You went home again?' she asked me through her chattering teeth.

Then she drank her chai down quickly, said her goodbyes and was off down the road. Through the rest of that last day of the Yatra, I caught sight of her a few more times. Fifty metres or so in front.

* * *

We ate a late lunch in Srinagar, on the Yatra's last full day of walking. As before, the dining hall was a large pandal, this time in a fenced-off field near the eastern shore of

Dal Lake. This being Kashmir, security was tighter than it had been in the other states. One of the yatris from the group I had been walking with stood near the gate, calling out names from a long list in his hand. Each one was frisked and passed through a metal detector, then they walked off towards lunch.

Me, I didn't see how my name would be called. While I knew these people by now, I was really just a hanger-on. So, I was getting set to go find lunch elsewhere. But Renuka shot down that plan: 'You're going to eat with us!' she said, firmly. To my astonishment, she was right: the man at the gate called my name. Who had thought to include me in this list? Renuka? She denied all responsibility.

After lunch, we walked out to the lake and relaxed on the shore. With no afternoon session, there was no more Yatra. The mood was simultaneously euphoric—think of what all these people had accomplished—and a little sad, for there were goodbyes ahead, and also that creeping thought, what next after a successful Yatra? Selfies were taken up and down that stretch of the lakeshore and swiftly distributed on WhatsApp. They are, against the overcast sky and the grey expanse of the lake, a riot of reds and browns, blues and yellows, and a wide array of smiles. Renuka is in several.

Renuka was the yatri I got to know best. She, too, had met my sister-in-law Ramani in Rajasthan and the two of them had connected immediately. That eased the way for me to get to know her. Though I also suspect it was her experience on the Yatra, as a whole, that allowed her to open up to others in ways that she might not otherwise have been allowed, growing up in small-town Madhya Pradesh. So sometimes by chance, sometimes on purpose,

Renuka and I ended up walking together a fair deal. When the Yatra ended in Srinagar's Lal Chowk, with everyone in high spirits and posing in large groups for photographs, Renuka made it a point to seek out and get a shot with each one of the friends she had made on the Yatra. Two at a time like that, in her album.

I particularly treasure the photograph of the two of us. She's in red shoes and what looks like a polka-dot kameez. I'm in my yellow winter jacket. Twin cut-outs of Rahul Gandhi are just visible over my right shoulder. Lal Chowk's famous clock tower rises above our heads, a flag on top. The place was simply buzzing that afternoon, people milling about in every direction. Yet whoever took the photo managed inadvertently to find an angle from where only a few others are visible, all facing away. But the best part about the photograph is the large Indian flag that seems to sprout from my right shoulder. I know that particular flag well—Virender Singh walked with it every day, usually leading the civil society group that Renuka was part of, breaking off to do what became his trademark, greeting little kids on the roadside. He's a tall, broad man, and at the moment of this shot I knew just where he was, waving his flag. But the angle, again, means he is completely hidden behind Renuka and me. All that's left is this disembodied flag, aflutter as he waves.

I like that shot.

Earlier that day, Renuka told me about what she called the greatest moment of her young life. It was from a few days earlier, but she was still in a state of excitement, wonderstruck that it had happened to her. I was delighted for her and, to my surprise, actually a little envious. Cynic that I am, after all. But hold on, I'll return to that moment.

Renuka is thirty. She was born and brought up in Ghatiya, a small town in Ujjain district of Madhya Pradesh, about 25 km north of the city of Ujjain. She is the eldest of four children, all of whose names begin with 'R' (Reena, Ritesh and Rekha are the others). That may have to do, she told me with a chuckle, with her *dada* and *dadi*. Their names are Ramaji and Resham.

This eldest 'R' finished school in Ghatiya and then studied at Ujjain's Government Madhav Arts and Commerce College. She earned a BA there, and by 2016, an MA too, in sociology. It was her subject that got her interested in issues around her. In college and later, she organized various blood donation drives, and then camps in that fraught mid-2021 period when Covid-19 was resurgent and oxygen was in desperately short supply. She also found time to coach young kids in their schoolwork.

Pursuing these and other issues, she got to thinking hard about equality, dignity and justice. Particularly, the widespread erosion of those values. Particularly, the yawning gap between the lived experience of the genders. Particularly, the yawning gap between the lived experience of Scheduled Castes and Tribes (SC/ST) and higher castes. Ujjain district, she told me, has the largest SC population in Madhya Pradesh, and there are always incidents. 'To take out a *baraat*,' she said, 'we have to ask for police protection—so tell me, what is this *azaadi* we have?'

What could she do to fight these battles? Or at least, to bring these concerns some wider attention?

Came the Yatra, in 2022. 'I wanted to tell some big leader about all these things,' she told me, and here was her chance. For weeks though, the Yatra weaved through south India, and that was too far for this young woman

who said she had never—cue a look of pure astonishment

on my face—stepped out of her home state. But of course,

it eventually did enter Madhya Pradesh, and when it

reached Burhanpur, that's when she made up her mind.

What helped was that this was a *padyatra*—on foot—and as

she saw it, this was the first such since another Gandhi

had done one, several decades ago.

To start, she walked for a couple of days. Early on

2 December, via some women activists from the Congress

she had met, she got a chance to meet and walk with

Rahul Gandhi. She spoke to him about caste in Ujjain

and how the climate is increasingly anti-reservation. She

told him her belief that it's because the Congress has not

taken up caste issues seriously that the party has sunk so

low, electorally. Gandhi, she said, 'felt bad' listening to

her. She was glad for the chance to meet him, but even more, that he listened to her make her case.

Renuka's plan was actually to return home that day. After all, she had managed to speak to a 'big leader' about her concerns. Besides, the white clothes she was wearing had got soiled with some mud—still more reason to go home. But at the morning tea break, while she was asking around for a ride to where she could catch a bus to Ghatiya, she ran into a man she knew, Tarun Singh. He asked her, 'Why are you going home? You've met only Rahul Gandhi. Why not meet the others on the Yatra?' He said, 'This is a life yatra, not just a padyatra.' When she pointed to her muddy clothes, he waved it off. 'Walk like that,' he said. 'You'll be hailed as a yatri who doesn't care about sweat, dirt or your appearance.'

Renuka was tempted. She walked some more that morning, then had lunch with several women on the Yatra. That's when she began to understand that this was not a purely Congress operation, because these women were not Congress workers. And this was good to know. So Renuka walked on till day's end, and by then was convinced. She actually did return home that night, but only for a day, and of course she had to change out of her muddy kameez. With two changes of clothes and Rs 500, she caught up with the Yatra again. Again though, she saw it as a short stint: walk till the Rajasthan border and return home.

But this time, she found a travelling home with civil society yatris, because the Congress groups were focused more on party activists. This group stood for whole sections of society—NGOs, academics, journalists, urban professionals and more—who want their voices heard, individually and collectively. In the past, governments have tapped such groups for their particular experience and expertise. But that happens far less now. That's why, like many others, they were on the Yatra.

At some point, Renuka got Yogendra Yadav, leader of the civil society group, to speak to her father, who was worried about her travels. Yadav put her father's mind at ease. 'If she's with you,' he told Yadav, 'she can go anywhere!' Just so did this young woman from Ghatiya finally set foot outside her home state. She stayed with the Yatra and the civil society folks, as it made its way through Rajasthan, then Delhi and briefly into Uttar Pradesh, Haryana, Punjab and finally Jammu and Kashmir. And through those weeks, Yadav 'took care of me like his own daughter'.

In the civil society group, but also in the Yatra in general, there were people of all kinds: poor, rich, from all over the country and even other political parties, even heart patients. There were writers, activists and professors. Renuka was surprised to find many walkers spending their own money—on transport, hotels, food—to be part of the Yatra. That told her something about what it meant to them.

Early on, Yadav handed Renuka the responsibility for the group's banner. She and a varying cast of others would unfurl it at the start of every walking stint. Holding it, they would lead the group out on to the road as slogans rang out behind. She loved the slogans: 'Nafrat chhodo, Bharat Jodo!' [Give up hate, heal India!] was one that resonated most, but there were others. 'Hum desh jodne nikle hain, aao hamare saath chalo!' [We're out to heal the country, come walk with us!], and 'Anekta mein ekta wala Bharat hamein *pyara hai!'* [We love the India of unity in diversity!]; and then there was the variation that would ring out in the early mornings: *'Bistar chhodo, Bharat Jodo!'* [Get out of bed, heal India!].

Like many others, Renuka was struck by the reception Rahul Gandhi got from ordinary people everywhere. In fact: 'The women who came up and embraced him,' she asked, 'are they mad? I spoke to many of them! They had never embraced any man apart from husbands or sons. But they didn't think of this as embracing a man. To them, Rahul was like a son.' After all, they told Renuka, here was someone, after so long, willing to listen.

And this, for Renuka, was the great success of the Yatra: that because they were being listened to, people had started speaking up about issues they had too long sidelined. 'People are starting to ask, what's right, what's wrong?'

The banner was a great honour. But there was more to come. On Republic Day, 26 January, the Yatra was to resume after being stalled by an avalanche the previous day. But first, there was a flag to be hoisted at the camp where the civil society members had spent the night. At 10.00 a.m., everyone gathered for the ceremony. Yogendra Yadav announced that there would be three flag-hoisters: Michael, their foreign guest over the previous few days; Pratyush Baba, at nearly seventy the oldest walker (but as I saw for myself, easily the most indefatigable), and the youngest—Renuka.

'When he called my name,' Renuka told me over lunch on the last day, 'my eyes and heart filled up so much, I had no words.' I don't know about her heart, but her eyes filled up once more, right there in front of me. In this beautiful part of the country, filled with meaning ('*Bharat ka swarg,*' she said, India's heaven), this group, now all her firm friends, gave

Renuka this singular honour. 'I started to weep.'

She called her father a little later. He started to weep

too. 'We are people from a small village,' he told her.

'We've not even stepped out of this district. Yet Yogendra-

ji gave you this chance.'

'You did the Yatra physically,' her father told her that

day. 'I did it with you, in my thoughts.'

* * *

Yogendra Yadav did his share of writing from the Yatra.

One article is a good-natured muse on 'selfie-attacks'

during those months: 'Often it is a group attack. They

surround me but are not sure who is going to take the

photo. As they find a volunteer and array themselves,

out comes a selfie arm in the middle, spoiling everyone else's frame.'[6]

Walking with Yadav, I saw this first-hand plenty of times. Once was during the midday rest stop somewhere in Rajasthan. I was lying on a mattress, trying to decide between a quick nap and going next door to get some lunch. Suddenly, there were a dozen or more men and a lone woman, standing around me. Yadav was among them, but this was one of his selfie-attacks, and so I had a unique ground-level view as it happened. So my own photographs of the moment are all elongated bodies

---

[6] Yogendra Yadav, 'This is what surprises me about India's selfie-hunters on Bharat Jodo Yatra, political events', Print, November 18, 2022, https://theprint.in/opinion/this-is-what-surprises-me-about-indias-selfie-hunters-on-bharat-jodo-yatra-political-events/1223216/ (accessed October 2, 2023).

and stretched arms—arms that end in carefully held smartphones. Yadav smiles through it all.

* * *

I had reason to feel kindly towards Neelotpal. Nearing Lalsot in Rajasthan, this tall young man in glasses was striding along beside me. His pace itself pushed me to speed up slightly—*was I going to let a young upstart upstage me? Never!* We didn't exchange a word, though, until—like so often—the next break for chai. That time, we were sitting together on a *charpai*, one of those that are already low and strung so loosely that you sink even lower into it. Couple that with the stiffness from three hours walking, and I drank my chai wondering whether I would be able to rise at all, let alone fight off possible upstages.

But Neelotpal and I introduced ourselves and spoke about this and that, particularly his once-membership in, and current disillusionment with, the Communist Party of India (CPI). Later, I got back to walking before he did. But just as I was getting into my rhythm again, he ran up from behind and fell in beside me. 'I didn't realize till I looked you up on Google—I've actually read one of your books!' he exclaimed.

Yes, I felt very kindly.

Neelotpal was a *Pradesh Yatri* and wore a badge around his neck that said as much. The label meant he was part of the Yatra while it was in the state—the fourteen days in Rajasthan, in this case. Speaking to him on the phone, months later, he told me how he got selected to be a Pradesh Yatri. 'I applied, and there were three days of tests,' he said, and I thought: 'Three days! That's some rigour in selection!' But as I was about to ask what the three days of testing involved, he said: 'All of us who had applied were interviewed, and it took three days to finish the interviews.' Ah. Not quite the impression I first had in my mind. His own interview, on the second day, lasted just minutes. An 'ex-army' man asked him, it's fourteen days in Rajasthan, do you think you will be able to walk?

Neelotpal said 'yes' and just like that—so he says—he was Pradesh Yatri #553 of about 2000 thus selected in Rajasthan. To be fair, he noted that some of the others did have more rigorous interviews, particularly after they seemed a little unsure of their ability to walk 25 km a day for fourteen days. But Neelotpal's immediate confidence spoke well for him.

So yes, Neelotpal was in the Communist Party 'long back'. I interrupted to ask, 'How long ago do you mean?' In his second year in college, 2019. 'Not that long ago!' I protested. 'Oh no,' said Neelotpal. 'When you're twenty-five years old, four years is a long time!' Hard to argue that point. In any case, at that time he saw himself as a 'hardline Marxist-Leninist' and felt an 'intellectual attachment' to the CPI. What he meant was, he was not temperamentally an activist but felt an ideological thread connected him and the party.

Only, once he joined the party, that connection crumbled: 'I changed completely to a total anti-communist.' What were his reasons? The communists, he found, were stuck in a time warp of their own making, borrowed from far-off countries and long-ago texts. They had no idea of the India of today, nor how to tailor their thinking to the India of today. Theirs was an ideology based on books, and those too dating 'from the 1840s!' In no way was it relevant in the India of the twenty-first century. His six months as a member cured him of his 'hardline' Marxism.

I couldn't help asking: for him, was it the ideology that was at fault? Or was it the party that did not adhere to, or advance, the ideology? In other words, could Marxism indeed be relevant in India today? 'Well, anything can be made relevant,' Neelotpal replied, 'if people are open and willing to adapt. But that may not be Marxism.'

So how would he, this lapsed and disillusioned Marxist, characterize his thinking today? In line with the ideas of Mohandas Gandhi and Jawaharlal Nehru, he said. They crafted a broadly liberal, secular nationalism. Unfortunately, that has been warped over the years. According to him, Indira Gandhi tried to 'compromise with the communists' when she was Prime Minister, and that ruined the ideology that shaped the freedom struggle. He is drawn to figures such as Ram Manohar Lohia and Jayaprakash Narayan, for the socialism—not communism—that they articulated. These were 'arch nationalists', not influenced by goings-on in Vietnam or Cuba, but by entirely Indian concerns: 'Garib aadmi hai, usko roti de do pehle' [If there's a poor man, give him something to eat first]. For Neelotpal, this reflects Gandhi's view of the poor and how the country should treat them: 'Gandhi was the most revolutionary of all our leaders.'

In any event, when he moved away from communism, Neelotpal naturally gravitated towards the Congress, even though today's Congress is 'not Gandhian at all'. He sees himself, therefore, as only a 'tactical supporter' of the party. It's in that context, if you like, that he first heard about the Bharat Jodo Yatra. As an effort at mass contact, it seemed very Gandhian to him, and the first effort like that in a very long time. Besides, the Yatra made a point of suggesting that if you were not part of any group, you were welcome to join up as individuals. That was another reminder of Gandhi and his focus on individual action and change.

All of which was part of Neelotpal's decision to join the Yatra on the night it entered Rajasthan, ready to walk for the next fourteen days. How ready? He had with him his phone, a book and a notebook, a few clothes, a water bottle and some dry fruit. Which book? Lucius Annaeus Seneca's *Letters from a Stoic*.

Quite a choice, for leisure reading while walking 300-plus km! But an inspired one. At the end of his third day on the Yatra, it was a very cold night—December in Rajasthan—his sandals were ruined, and his legs and feet were in pain from the unfamiliar exertions. He turned that night to Seneca's letters. One suggested that real terror comes from thinking about your problem. Don't, and the problem shrinks. 'We suffer more often in imagination than in reality,' wrote Seneca.

That night, 'his book gave me great solace,' Neelotpal said—and after that, the rest of his time on the Yatra went smoothly.

Not that this tactical supporter was pleased with everything about the Yatra. On his second day, for example, he found that a number of local Congress leaders had arrived to join it, all in their cars and wanting to travel in them, and yet all desperate to be seen with Rahul Gandhi. In that moment, he saw some truth in what he called the *darbari* culture that the Congress is often accused of nurturing: that some members of the party want only to get close to the leaders and keep others away.[7]

---

[7] See for example this report from when Jaiveer Shergill quit the party in 2022: https://timesofindia.indiatimes.com/videos/news/jaiveer-shergill-slams-darbari-culture-within-congress-after-ghulam-nabi-azads-resignation/videoshow/93807359.cms (accessed 5 October 2023).

But there were also people who had been in the party for years who were simply walking, not trying to be noticed in any way. That spirit was encouraging. 'Nobody talks about the party's devoted cadre,' Neelotpal said. Particularly moving was eighty-eight-year-old Karuna Prasad Mishra, bent over but walking steadily. On one of those days in Rajasthan, Mishra's bag was stolen. Neelotpal bought him a shawl.

All in all, the Yatra taught Neelotpal plenty about the diversity in his own state: the dialects, behaviours, food and more. It also changed his perspective on politics. He wants to be involved in some way—if not electorally, at least in activist politics.

I was left thinking about something else Seneca wrote: 'It is a rough road that leads to the heights of greatness.'

* * *

These are just a few examples, of many whom I met and walked with. In them, like in the rest, there was a nearly visible determination and purpose in manner, in their approach to the Yatra. In fact, to me that seemed almost the 'why' of their walking. That is, here they were, showing the world that there are still people motivated not by religious structures, not by past glories, not by hatreds deliberately stoked. No, these were ordinary folks doing something extraordinary purely because they think that effort might shake a nation out of a spiralling miasma of division, mistrust, cynicism, sophistry and violence. Some might disagree about the contours of that miasma, sure. Some might disagree that this Yatra will actually produce such shaking, certainly. But what's hard to disagree with is the simple, yet clear like the blue sky, sense of purpose in the folks participating in the Yatra.

And that's even before mentioning those who were not walking. Meaning, the crowds we passed everywhere: smiling, waving, wanting to shake hands, cheering. Babies in arms, adults in their most colourful clothes, kids squealing in delight as I photographed their colourful sandals, women who looked close to ninety . . . There's plenty to be said for perspective that time and distance allow, but right there and then, it was hard not to think that the Yatra was reaching out to touch Indians in unexpected ways. As another usually sceptical friend commented, 'Surprisingly, the Yatra seems to be making headway in the right direction!'

And Rahul Gandhi? As central as he was to the Yatra, there was also a sense that in the end, its real message was larger than him. Instead, it is about hope and optimism in India; in the India our remarkable Constitution promises.

So yes, what was the 'Bharat jodne ka plan' the Congress had?

As I saw it during the Yatra: first, stand up to those who would break this country. Second, listen fully and sincerely to people speak about their concerns: education, health, women's issues, jobs, inflation, whatever. Third, lay out the Congress's own plans to address such concerns. Its own vision for the country.

My impression is that the Congress did pretty well on the Yatra with the first two of those. The third needs more substance. To many of us, the Congress is a party struggling with its reason to exist, its relevance, its political decline over many years. That decline is a worry for anyone, like me, who values democracy. But at least it's struggling—meaning its members are not complacent, apathetic or dispirited.

As a plan, I'll take that. For me, that was the exhilarating, uplifting thing about the Yatra.

5

On the Inside: This Walker Looks Around

When I wanted to run in the Mumbai Marathon a few years ago, it was pretty much impossible to run simply because . . . you wanted to. Instead, runners had to register through one NGO or another, and use the Marathon to raise funds for it. That is, run for a cause. Not merely for yourself. To be honest, this never quite made sense to me. I believe the Marathon organizers should welcome both kinds of runners.

The first time I joined the Bharat Jodo Yatra, I heard faint echoes of that marathon experience. Our little group could simply turn up and walk. Or we could see this as a chance to tell a political party our concerns about certain issues in our country: not quite walking for a cause, but close.

We chose the latter. Unlike at the Marathon, we had the choice.

Six of us formed that group, to join the Yatra that first time. I've mentioned them before: there was my brother Ravi and sister-in-law Ramani, both doctors trained in community health who have worked for many years in rural India. There were two of their colleagues, Prasanna and Guru. These are not doctors, but are concerned with health care in different ways—advocacy, training and the like. Two journalists—one of them Shivam, the other me—rounded out our little team.

When we met in Bengaluru and started working our way to KB Cross in Karnataka's Tumakuru district, where we planned to climb to the Yatra bandwagon, it struck me how strangely fitting a team we had formed. Not only were we from disparate professions and paths in life. Not only were some of us meeting and travelling together for the first time. But none of us belonged to the Congress in any sense. In fact, some of us were cynical about the Yatra, and had actually been vocal critics of Rahul Gandhi and the Congress in the past. Take me: in 2013, I wrote an article about him that ended with these lines: '[Gandhi] cannot find the fibre to meet his people. And yet some speak of him as a future prime minister. Oh what a fall was this, my countrymen!'

Yet something about this Yatra had called to us all, had overcome the cynicism. We wanted to stand up against hatred, make a statement about the current regime. That call was the thread that ran through all six of us.

And in a very real sense, we were typical of so many who were on the Yatra. The thread ran through so many of so many different persuasions.

Start with the core of the Yatra—members of the Congress Party. Some of them were advisers to Rahul Gandhi. Others were politicians or party activists. An entire troop of volunteers of the Seva Dal, a Congress outfit, would lead the Yatra out every morning, wearing white and working up a serious pace. I know that pace first-hand, because I fell in with them once, in Rajasthan. Usually, right behind them were the smartly dressed musicians who formed a marching band, playing patriotic songs as they marched. Then came the civil society group, in yellow sweaters and jackets, especially as we travelled ever further north. Prominent among them was the academic and politician Yogendra Yadav—like me, once a strident Congress critic. And then there were those in the inner circle—not necessarily close to Gandhi, but people walking inside the moving island that was defined by rope that a posse of smart police constables held.

And that's not all either. All the time, there were people lining the road and cheering, or chanting slogans. They came out in large numbers everywhere, but I particularly remember Punjab.

The evening we walked into Khanna, we were on the service road of NH-44. This is the ancient Grand Trunk Road, and so there were moments when I caught myself actually thinking of the 2500 years of history below my feet. Anyway, in this stretch through Khanna, the highway itself was above us. Every hundred metres or so, we walked past an underpass built to allow access to the other side of the highway. These were of particular interest to me, because the hotel I was to spend the night in—the one where Rimpy had dropped off my backpack—was some distance on the other side of the highway. So at some point, I had to peel off from the Yatra and make my way through to the other side.

Only, every successive underpass was so jam-packed that I couldn't hope to push through. Each time, I looked at the crowd and thought, 'Naah, I'll try the next one.' We passed several like this. So many, that when I finally found one with space enough for me, I was well beyond the road on the other side that led to my hotel. Already stiff and exhausted from the day's exertions, in some pain from blisters on my feet, and now deprived of the adrenaline of being on the Yatra, it was a serious struggle to limp those 3 km or so to the hotel.

Not that I'm complaining. Because those underpasses were packed with people come out to see us, to greet us. They were singing, chanting slogans. They were honking scooter horns, blowing whistles, I even saw one man blowing a conch. They were reaching out to give us water, sweets, to just shake hands with us. I couldn't get over this exuberant curiosity, this hearty, full-throated welcome. Sure, I couldn't get through it, but I didn't mind because in truth, I couldn't get enough of it.

The next day, more of the same as our civil society group, ahead of the main Yatra, approached Ludhiana. There were stages with blaring music and bhangra dancers in gleaming costumes. Several dozen schoolkids in rows.

Their teachers also lined up, holding up signs to welcome us. A young woman with a mike, leading a whole orchestra in slogans. Workers from a factory, uniformed executives from a car dealership. At one point, several dozen women sitting on tiered stands, clapping and cheering us on. And when we reached Samrala Chowk, where we were to stop for the day and where I was to peel off again to find my driver, the crowd waiting for us was, I could hardly believe it, even larger, even noisier, even more boisterous than anything before.

In that melee, someone to my left tapped my shoulder to ask me something. I turned to speak to him for what must have been no more than a couple of minutes. Done, I turned back. To my astonishment, I could no longer see any of my civil society comrades, none of the yellow jackets they were all wearing. Not one. They were somewhere in that mass of humanity, but I had no idea in which direction they had gone. Left with no choice, I pushed my way through the crowd and started trying to work out how to meet my driver. The same feeling as Khanna the previous day: adrenaline gone, blisters and stiffness now my companions.

Still not complaining, though.

Ludhiana was exceptional and exhilarating, but there had been high-spirited crowds in Rajasthan and Karnataka before, too, and it was something to see from the inside. People lining the streets, standing on rooftops, packing balconies, spilling out of gates. People running alongside the rope-carrying cops. People handing out luscious yellow bananas, or little sachets with nuts and slices of coconuts, or small water bottles with Yatra labels. The men on a truck giving anyone who asked a serving of *roti-sabzi*—'*do le lo bhai!'* (take two!) one said, and I was glad I took his advice. People somehow jumping into the island and trying to make their way to Rahul Gandhi, sometimes successfully. Photographs and videos showed us that walking in that inside zone through the course of the Yatra were women, men, girls, boys, Muslims, Christians, Hindus, rich, poor, academics, farmers, politicians, doctors, actors, film-makers, sanitation workers, the disabled . . .

The point? The Yatra drew absolutely no lines. Whatever your particular identity, or even if you claimed none, you were welcome. To walk yes, but also to gawk, to wave, to shout, to run alongside, to just stand there as the whole procession made its way past. You were very welcome.

* * *

The four public health folks in our group in Karnataka had prepared a short brief on issues, such as malnutrition and the right to health care. They wanted to speak about this to the Congress leaders during the Yatra. That actually happened. The pair of us journalists, though, were the ones without a cause. Which was fine with us. We wanted to walk and observe, that's all. So here's some of that. In particular, something about logistics.

To start, how were we to join the Yatra? You will have got a sense of that from earlier, with my experience in Ambala. Here's how it went in Karnataka.

There was a published schedule for the Yatra, according to which we had decided a location. But the schedule tended to change slightly every day. When we first picked 9 and 10 October as our dates, the Yatra website told us that the Yatra would start from Turuvekere on the

9th morning and walk some 40 km to Gubbi. The next day, it would trek on to Sira, another 55 km. These distances were daunting by themselves, but there were other obstacles to overcome before we could even think of walking all those kilometres. How would we reach Turuvekere by 6.30 a.m.? Where would we spend the night? Ideally, we'd have liked to stay with the Yatra, but they had no arrangements for bandwagon-hoppers like us. So if not in Turuvekere on the 8th night, and Gubbi on the 9th, where? How would we get there? How would we return to Gubbi by 6.30 a.m. the next day?

Taking everything into account, we worked out a plan that went like this. Reach Tumakuru on the 8th and spend the night there—someone kindly arranged for us to stay at the Tumkur Club. Hire a minibus to take us the 65 km to Turuvekere on the 9th morning, drop us just ahead of the Yatra and drive on to wait for us at Gubbi. End of the day, we'd climb back on the minibus and return to Tumakuru—20 km from Gubbi—to spend the night at the Club. On the 10th morning, take the minibus back to Gubbi, have it drive ahead again and wait for us at Sira. Return the 50 km to Tumakuru.

But of course, the Yatra's schedule was fluid, subject to change every day, as the website itself warned us. Those two days were no exception. Late on 8th October, we got the schedule for the 9th: the 6.30 a.m. start was not at Turuvekere, but at Kibbanahalli (KB) Cross, 50 km from Tumakuru. We'd walk all day till Ankanabavi—23 km. This was still doable from our Tumkur Club base. So we woke at 4.30 a.m. on the 9th and were on the road to KB Cross by 5 a.m.

Again, our contacts in the Yatra had suggested that the best place to walk would be a hundred metres or so in front of Rahul Gandhi. That would mean keeping his pace or better. If we didn't think that was possible, the next best would be a similar distance behind. Either way, we were told, we'd avoid being shoved around by the crowds jockeying for a glimpse of Gandhi. After plenty of discussion, our group chose the front. That meant we had to pass KB Cross before the Yatra started that day, station ourselves somewhere ahead and wait for it to catch up.

Which we did. And we waited. A small posse of yatris showed up at about 6.40 a.m., carrying a flag, waving fists aloft and chanting slogans. These were some of the Seva Dal volunteers. We let them pass. Another group, a little larger. We let them pass too. Then the marching band. Then suddenly, it was upon us—a river of men and women flowing down the road, kept in some apparent order by a large number of cops, some of whom held on to the long rope I mentioned that gives Gandhi safe space to walk. We tried to insinuate ourselves into the flood—'stay ahead, stay ahead!' was our mantra, after all—but it was a hopeless task. Before we knew it, we were floundering along on the edge, pushed this way and that by the crowd, just what we had hoped to avoid. Within minutes, and without fully comprehending how it came to be, we two journalists found ourselves plodding along far behind our colleagues, far behind the bulk of the Yatra, sharing the road not with walkers so much as a mess of honking, slow-moving vehicles.

Not the Yatra we had in mind.

Over the next half-hour, I struggled through the crowds—ecstatic young men mostly, shouting 'Rahul bhaiyya!' and 'Photo please!' as they ran for spells—to overtake the Yatra and get to the front. That's when the realization hit: the best spot to walk was just behind two press vehicles. They were jam-packed with reporters filming the Yatra, so they had to both keep pace with the yatris and stay in front. Perfect.

But all this planning and struggle took us only so far. Late that evening, still some distance short of the evening halt at Ankanabavi, Ravi found his shoes falling apart. So we stopped for the day. But our minibus was at Ankanabavi, and between us and that small metropolis was . . . the whole Yatra. For the minibus to reach us, we had to wait where we were—a cheery roadside chai shop—until the Yatra and all the traffic piled up behind it rolled not just past us, but past Ankanabavi.

Which waiting would have been all right, except that the chai shop ran out of milk after the first round of tiny cuppas. 'Too many customers!' said the woman running it. She didn't seem unhappy.

More logistical issues the next morning. The organizers had offered to take us into the cordon to meet Gandhi.

For which, they sent us a Google Maps pin locator for where they wanted us to wait: an Indane gas dealership several kilometres ahead of that day's kick-off point. This meant we had to get ahead of the Yatra at the start and make sure we were still ahead at the Indane dealership. This also meant a 4.00 a.m. wake-up, because the kick-off point for that morning was nearly 35 km ahead of the previous day's KB Cross start, thus more than 80 km from Tumakuru. Besides, we were not allowed bags inside the cordon, so those had to stay in our minibus.

It was touch-and-go, but we managed to reach the Yatra minutes before it started. We worked our way through the waiting throngs, got ahead and started walking. With some hiccups, we were all in place on time at Indane, bag-free and ready.

Except that when the Yatra got there, the previous group walking with Gandhi was still with him. So we fell in, once more, in step with the press trucks. About an hour and a tea break later, someone beckoned to us and we entered the cordon. 'No bags!' he said, pointing to the purple strap across my chest—the instruction we had already been given. But my strap belonged not to a bag but to my camera. 'Okay,' he said, 'but you cannot take any photographs.' I nodded as he shepherded us to the edge of the cordon, striding single-file alongside the line of rope-wielding constables for several more minutes. Then, to Gandhi's side.

All of which is what it took, to walk and talk with him for the next twenty minutes. And that's just for the few of us. The Yatra's logistical challenges for all its participants were, need I say it, far wider and more intricate than this much.

Consider how the organizers dealt with just two of them.

Take the posters and bunting that lined the route: Ambedkar, Gandhi, Sardar Patel, Bose and several other contemporary Congress-wallahs. When we were waiting, tea-deprived, short of Ankanabavi near the end of our first day, we saw a few young men uprooting posters and piling them on to a small truck. These were Tamil-speakers, hired in Kanyakumari to travel with the Yatra all the way to Kashmir. Their job: first, journey ahead of the Yatra, erecting posters on the route to the next break point. Second, allow the Yatra to trundle past. Third, follow it, picking up the posters. Repeat. Every single day, repeat.

Back-breaking work, but the men did a fine job. Driving north from KB Cross early on our second day, cruising the same route that we had trudged along only hours before, it was as if nothing had happened there only hours before. Not a single poster was left. 'There are about 250 of us,' one of the men told us, 'and they pay us Rs 1000 each per day.'

Take toilets. It's one thing to organize portable toilet facilities for the hundreds of yatris and add-ons like me. It's another thing altogether to maintain a certain degree of cleanliness in those toilets, enough said. I've been at plenty of public gatherings where it takes courage and the ability to stop breathing for a spell, even to step into their toilets. What did the Yatra have in store for those of us seeking to relieve ourselves?

At the midday halt on our second day, I walked up to the portable toilet in some trepidation. It was a large truck carrying a large container, steps at the back leading into the container. Already holding my breath, I climbed the little staircase—into immediate wonder.

It was spotless. It was odourless. It was largely dry. There were two large Parryware sinks set on a granite countertop, fitted with stylish Jaquar taps. The commodes and urinals were Parryware too, spotless too. There were bottles of handwash, a bottle of sanitizer on a stand in the corner. And if all that was startling enough, there was a cherry on top. On the counter, a small vase with, I could hardly believe it, flowers.

I mean, this was a scene, no exaggeration, out of some high-class hotel.

There's plenty to say about the progress of the Bharat Jodo Yatra, about Rahul Gandhi's meetings with people and groups including ours, about the surging crowds, about the brisk pace the Yatra kept up, day after day, month after month. All that says things—about the Congress, our politics, the issues our country faces and more.

But spare a thought, too, for everything that went on behind the scenes, logistically, to keep the Yatra on the road; for the ways people on the Yatra connected with people outside it. Because all that says something too.

6

Hope: What It Kindles

It was impossible to walk on the Yatra without speculations and discussions about what it was achieving and was meant to achieve. To be sure, with every new acquaintance, there were the exchanges prompted by questions such as 'Where have you come from?' and 'Why have you joined?' and 'How long have you been walking?' and 'How long do you plan to walk?' and the like. But after working through all that, the conversation turned naturally towards the purpose of the Yatra.

What was its purpose, anyway? I mean, no doubt its organizers in the Congress Party had clearly defined goals, maybe even broken down by state and district. But what about participants? How did they—we, I—see the Yatra? What did I see as its purpose, as distinct from my own purpose?

In answering such questions, the first thing I had to comprehend fully was that this was, in the end, a political act. That may not be saying much, given that the Yatra was organized and peopled by a political party. But what I'm getting at is politics beyond party happenings. This was politics more elemental, more stripped-down, more basic. This was politics in how people meet and talk and exchange ideas—maybe disagreeing—about their society, how it is governed and how it should be governed.

And as far as I could tell, exactly that was happening up and down the long columns of yatris and hangers-on. Just being on the Yatra set off thoughts and talk in plenty of directions: the state of the country, the state of the Congress, upcoming elections, the possibility of a second Yatra going west to east, the need for some opposition unity, like that.

Like one afternoon, when a number of us had Kashmir on our minds. Not surprising, because as the Yatra wound its way ever further north, Kashmir became a steadily larger chunk of our conversations.

Some eight or ten of us climbed into a van to go have lunch with a local farmer. We had been walking all morning, it was now pretty hot and we were hungry as well. Thus the almost palpable hope in the van, that it would be a quick ride to the farm and that lunch would be hot and tasty as Rajasthan is known for. As we travelled, somebody brought up the end of the Yatra, then about a month-and-a-half away and as things stood that day, to happen in Kashmir. Why discuss that finish line now? Why here, in Rajasthan? Because it was no longer some almost indefinite number of weeks in the future. If the Yatra kept its schedule—and so far, it essentially had—the finish line was now starting to loom into view.

So the Yatra would reach Kashmir—or more correctly, the new administrative units of what used to be the state of Jammu and Kashmir. But how would things go, in those units? (For convenience, I'll refer to them from now on as simply 'Kashmir'. After all, that's how it figured in our conversations.)

In over three months, through nearly a dozen entries the Yatra made into different Indian states, there had been no serious problems, whether of security or food or something else. The Congress might have been better organized in one or the other state, or there might have been doubts about police and administrative support in states ruled by other parties. But by and large, these concerns didn't turn into handicaps. There were hiccups, but the Yatra had rolled along with an admirable order and sure-footedness.

Would Kashmir be any different? There was reason to ask that question. To begin, India has stationed several hundred thousand soldiers in that state. No other Indian state has anything similar, or even close to similar. The presence of that many armed men, and for many years now, gives words like 'normal' and 'security' whole new meanings in Kashmir. So the first question was: would the Yatra even enter Kashmir? That was always the plan, but would some reality nobody had anticipated now set in and force the Yatra to wind up at the Punjab-Kashmir border? Possible, but that didn't seem likely to any of us.

What did seem likely was some curtailment of the Yatra—not in distance or route, but in the number of people walking. For we could imagine that state's authorities raising the question of 'security' and finding nods of agreement in other corners of the country. How, they might ask, is it possible to ensure the safety of hundreds, possibly thousands, of walkers—let alone Rahul Gandhi—in a state that has seen so many random attacks, so much violence?

Nods of agreement on reading those words? Only, that particular worry could also apply to other states the Yatra had traversed. Punjab saw years of internecine violence in the 1980s and 1990s. Maharashtra witnessed weeks of bloodletting in 1992-93 that killed over a thousand Indians. Delhi was where some 3000 Indians were slaughtered in 1984 solely because they wore turbans, and in early 2020, our capital was convulsed in days of violence that killed several dozen. If the Yatra's thousands had walked the highways, through the villages and cities of those states, all without incident—well, what made Kashmir special?

Still, in the van that day, we spoke of such curtailment. Some of us had heard from the organizers about limiting the number who would walk in Kashmir. What that number was, was just guesswork now. A few dozen? 200? Whatever it was, who would decide the names? I had no illusions—I was the hanger-on, the last priority to get on to any such list. So if all this was more than just rumours, I would give up any hope of walking in Kashmir.

There was time for those considerations, of course. For now, our discussion that day went beyond just the question of what shape the Yatra would take in Kashmir. How would it be received there, by the people of the state?

Again, it must say something about Kashmir and our perception of it that this was something to wonder about. Again, there was no other state that had us wondering how the Yatra would be received by its people. But Kashmir? Think of all we've been fed over the years, about widespread anti-India feeling there. That most Kashmiris are hostile to Indians. That they don't even consider themselves Indian.

But I also wondered, why was I myself thinking so much about Kashmir as I walked? Creeping into my mind whenever I wasn't talking to someone, an earlier trip to that state.

* * *

That was in 2004, during that year's Lok Sabha election. Four of us drove around and outside Srinagar, visiting polling booths and trying to get a sense of the mood. That day had left a lasting impression.

Armed men were a constant presence, in large numbers, at each booth where we stopped. Typically, there would be one set of men at the entrance. These men would check our IDs. Another set was deployed outside the rooms where the voting happened.

In most locations in rural areas outside the city of Srinagar, there was steady voting in progress. Lines of voters, divided into men and women, were waiting patiently to vote. Only an hour or so after polling opened, several booths we visited had recorded 10 per cent and more turnout.

We expected about the same at a booth outside Ganderbal, for example. But that's where we met a whole lot of eligible voters who had turned up but were refusing to vote. One man told me rather firmly: 'We won't vote until our issues are addressed. The whole world knows what Kashmir's situation is. We don't want this atmosphere of guns, we want peace.' As if on cue, a jawan from the Rashtriya Rifles (RR) came up to ask who I was and what I was doing. This soldier seemed inquisitive and friendly, and we exchanged a few pleasantries—until a fellow jawan called him away. I could hear this second jawan and a superior RR officer, both visibly annoyed, asking the first man testily why he had been speaking to me.

Still, the overall impression from the rural booths was of a quiet election with a steady stream—not a fast-flowing one, okay—of voters. Shopkeepers, though, had observed a call for a boycott that had gone out the previous day: in nearly every village, they had shut for the day.

But 'steady stream' was not the phrase that came to mind when we roamed the city itself. The boycott call was clearly being observed by nearly everyone. All shops were shut, the streets were nearly deserted. That is, apart from people playing cricket and, in two cases, chess and carrom. In booth after booth, we found almost nobody voting, and almost nobody had voted, either. At a booth on Ali Kadal, for example, of 930 people listed, zero had turned up. And this was at 1.30 p.m., several hours after it had opened. In Shivpora and Rajbagh, upper-class areas of the city that we also visited, of about 4000 names on the rolls, less than fifty had voted. And this was well after 4.00 p.m., only a couple of hours before the polls closed.

Elsewhere, a group of men explained the poor turnout to us, getting increasingly heated and nearly gheraoing us. 'Since 1989,' one said, 'we have decided not to vote, and we will keep this up until there is some *faisla* here. These elections have brought us nothing! We will keep up these boycotts until we get *azaadi*.' Political parties, another said, were populated solely by 'thieves and international crooks'. Several kept shouting in my face that they did not want to be with 'Hindustan'. So I asked, are you for Pakistan then? To my astonishment, there was a unanimous and angry 'No!' They had, if it could be called that, even more contempt for Pakistan. 'We just want Kashmir to be free!' they said. 'From both these countries!'

Sentiments like these were in the air everywhere we went in Srinagar. But we also heard plenty of talk of *aman* (peace). Any number of people came up to speak of their weariness of years of violence, the oppressive security presence, of a yearning for peace.

But through it all, what was obvious to us, all that day, was the resistance many Kashmiris felt to the electoral process and thus to Indian democracy itself. There was also, though, fear. Of the security forces, of course. But of others as well. One man wanted to remain anonymous, and asked, 'What if someone spots me going to vote and reports me to the boycott-wallahs? Will they target me?'

The point? Few people we met that election day were satisfied with India and our democracy.

* * *

Of course, it has been nineteen years, nearly two decades since that day. Of course, my experience there was during an election, a far from normal time anywhere, let alone Kashmir. But on the Yatra, I couldn't shake those memories. Couldn't help speaking about them, if sketchily, to some of my walking mates. Couldn't help wondering if this was going to be the climate in which the Yatra would enter Kashmir. So in the van, when one of my colleagues—he had clearly been mulling thoughts like these over as well—said we need to tread carefully in that state, he triggered a spirited debate.

'What do you mean by "carefully"?' I asked him.

His point was, there are strong feelings in Kashmir. There are enough people hostile to India—leave aside their feelings towards Pakistan—whom a large procession like this would only provoke. Did the Yatra really want to do that? Wouldn't it be better to keep a low profile?—that's if we entered Kashmir at all. That is, have only a token band of yatris enter the state and walk without fanfare. Maybe even a token walk. Meaning, get to Srinagar by other means—rail, road, air—and parade down one of its boulevards. Certainly not Lal Chowk, with the significance that spot carries for so many Kashmiris. Certainly no flag-raising, there or elsewhere.

It was something to consider, no doubt. No doubt there's a history to remember and maybe—yes—tread carefully around. There's been too much mistrust for too long. The Congress itself has much to answer for in that state and can hardly expect to be greeted without wariness at best. Keeping all that in mind, why push buttons that are somewhat settled for now, forgive the clumsy metaphor?

But there's another way to look at this, and another of our colleagues in the van explained that perspective.

It begins with the name of the Yatra itself, he said. 'Bharat Jodo', after all. The goal is to heal this country, to bring it together. Surely that must include the wounds in Kashmir, the years of violence and tragedy, the cruel exodus of Kashmiri Pandits and more? In fact, how can this healing happen—what can it possibly mean—if we sidestep Kashmir? There are ways in which that state, for better or worse, wittingly or not, shapes our identity as Indians. The Yatra seeks to reclaim a certain idea of what it means to be Indian that's been battered too long. What would it serve to turn away from arguably the stiffest test in that effort?

But there's more, too. The BJP's great triumph, this colleague explained, was that it has been able to capture and shape narratives of Indian patriotism and nationalism. They proclaim what those ideas are made of, and the rest of us are left playing catch-up. I don't like their articulation of nationalism, but why do I only react to it, instead of articulating my own vision? With Kashmir, the BJP and its ideological mates have always made a virtue of flying the Indian tricolour in Srinagar's Lal Chowk. Murli Manohar Joshi did it in 1992, for example. This act, we were encouraged to believe, needed a 'courage' that few others in the country possess. In fact, raising the Indian flag anywhere else in the country, we must assume the BJP signals to us, doesn't require the same courage and is not worth taking note of in the same way anyway. That itself should say things about Kashmir.

But if we who don't care for the BJP's political antics choose not to fly the flag in Lal Chowk, not to rock the boat that is our apparent consensus on Kashmir, we cede the argument to the BJP. They will lose no time in reducing the Yatra's message to this one empty platitude: that these

Bharat Jodo yatris are afraid to raise the Indian flag in Kashmir, thus they are un-Indian, even anti-Indian. All over again, the BJP sets the narrative and is able to slot its critics where the BJP itself chooses.

For those reasons, our friend in the van said, it was crucial not to shy away from Kashmir. Maybe the Yatra will step on some Kashmiri toes, and those should be attended to. But it also had to treat Kashmir as just another Indian state the Yatra had traversed, such as Kerala or Maharashtra or Haryana. Anything else, and detractors would have handed to the BJP a stick to beat the Yatra with.

I could see his logic, and I certainly did not want to hand the BJP any sticks. But I also wanted to keep in mind—for the Yatra to keep in mind—that Kashmir has, as someone I know remarked, 'never been like any other Indian state, not socially, not administratively, not constitutionally'. Troops are visible everywhere there, unlike in other states. But even other than that, Article 370 of the Indian Constitution allowed Kashmir a separate constitution. It gave to the Government of India power over the state only in matters of communication, defence and foreign affairs. That Article was abrogated in 2019, of course—but the point about Kashmir being different remains.

In any case, my colleague didn't know yet what the Yatra's organizers had in mind for Kashmir. But he believed the best course would be to enter the state in numbers, like everywhere else, walk to Srinagar, raise the Indian flag at Lal Chowk and hold a public meeting. That is, stick to the original plan and vision for the Yatra.

But in doing so in Kashmir in particular, he advised, the Yatra should not lose its greatest appeal and purpose:

listen to the ordinary people who come out to meet and greet us. To my ears, he was suggesting that any disaffection we notice among Kashmiris has its roots in our persistent unwillingness to listen to them, in assuming things about them and their ideas. The Yatra offered hope for something different instead: just listen.

He wasn't just optimistic that this approach would succeed. He seemed certain that this approach would appeal to Kashmiris, overcome doubts and scepticism about India in that state, overcome the distrust of Kashmiris that so many Indians seem to feel. Optimistic? Maybe. But it was, to him, imperative that the Yatra go to Kashmir.

'We have to reclaim the narrative,' he said.

Tread carefully, versus reclaim the narrative. What would the Yatra do?

* * *

For me, the Yatra's climax in Kashmir was the coming to fruition of everything it stirred up and promised as it traversed the country. That may be stating the obvious, but it meant something to me. It gave shape to a sense of hope that had been growing through the previous weeks, if amorphously.

The Yatra had faced at least one serious obstacle as it made its way through Kashmir. On the highway to Srinagar, there was an avalanche. Halted in their tracks, the Yatris had to return to where they had spent the previous night, unsure of whether they would be able to proceed the next day. There were also stories of an uncontrolled crowd of onlookers flooding the route of the Yatra, making Rahul Gandhi's security detail uneasy.

Meanwhile, allegations and counter allegations flew about. Had the state police not provided enough security to the Yatra? Police officials denied this, claiming their arrangements were foolproof and implying that the Yatra organizers were themselves responsible for any perception of danger. As for the avalanche, at least one TV news crew made its way to the point on the highway where the Yatra had been stopped. Picking his way past earth-moving equipment and over some rubble on the road, the reporter arrived at the mouth of a tunnel and pointed out to his viewers that it was clear. Why then, he asked, had the Yatra been stopped? There was nothing really to hinder their progress to and through the tunnel, and thence on to Srinagar. His visuals only underlined this apparently clear passage.

Watching all this from Bombay, having just made my Srinagar travel plans for a few days later, I began to worry. Would the Yatra actually reach Srinagar? Would it be forced to stop somewhere short of the city? If so, how would I make contact with them? Should I cancel my trip altogether?

It turned out that the Yatra did indeed resume its journey the next day. Having lost a day of walking, the yatris took buses to make up the miles. I held on to my ticket to Srinagar for later that week and took the flight when the day came.

In Srinagar, I faced a far less serious obstacle, but an obstacle nevertheless: the familiar 'how do I reach the kick-off point for the day?' I had got in touch with another walker, who was planning, like me, to rejoin the Yatra for its last full day of walking. She was oddly vague about how she was going to do it. Still, we decided to meet early at a bakery on the outskirts of the city, only a few minutes' walk from her hotel, and make our way together from there to where the Yatra would start from that day. As far as we could tell, a long stretch of road led straight from the bakery to that point.

Getting to the bakery that morning was already a nearly 3-km walk for me. As soon as I reached, my phone buzzed. It was the woman I was supposed to meet. 'I took a rickshaw,' she said. With police cordons blocking off all traffic along the route the Yatra was to take, her rickshaw must have had to do a wide detour. She could still have come by the bakery and picked me up—no restrictions on that road—but had blithely chosen not to. In fact, she now was, she said, a long way beyond where I stood and there was no way to return for me. In some frustration and anger, I disconnected and started evaluating my options.

That was cut short by three men walking towards me. Obviously yatris, and I even remembered the one carrying an Indian flag from my time in Rajasthan, when we had walked side by side for an hour or so. I fell in with them. 'Six to eight kilometres to walk,' one said. 'One hour. We'll make it in time.' If I didn't quite share it, I certainly admired his confidence, but it required an effort to keep pace with them. Twice, journalists wanted to speak to us. We did so without breaking stride, the man holding up his phone to capture us on video, scrambling backwards at speed. I was grateful for the break when we met Jahnavi over tea. By then, though, we had walked far enough, fast enough, that I was also sure we'd be in time for the Yatra.

At one point, I asked to carry the flag for a while. To my astonishment, the very act had tears welling up in my eyes. So only hours later, when I listened to Renuka speak about her experience with the flag just days before, I understood her emotions only too well.

Not long after I handed the flag back, we were there. The Yatra was just starting to move. I walked past the Seva Dal volunteers in starched whites, some of them waving and smiling. Past the marching band, every bit as smart and energetic as before. Caught sight of the civil society banner ...

... 'Hello Dilip,' said Yogendra Yadav from behind the banner. 'Welcome home.'

The tears, once more.

* * *

I fell in with the Yatra. We walked back, nearly all the 'six to eight kilometres'. Many more bystanders out on the road. A group of women in elegant *pherans*, one carrying a platter of sweets, actually stopped us. Some were weeping. Made the rounds of the women in our group, hugging them. Offered the sweets all round. 'Thank you for coming,' they said, over and over again. 'Today is the first day since 2019 we've come out so freely,' said one, referring to the abrogation of Article 370. 'Nobody'—and she pointed to a small group of armed soldiers nearby—'asked where we were going.' To my surprise, one of the soldiers even nodded slightly. Picking different listeners from among us, they spoke as if a dam had broken, the words almost tripping over themselves, the emotion visible. For at least half an hour, we were halted there, just listening.

The scene repeated, with another group of pheran-clad women, about half a kilometre ahead.

'Thank you for listening.' One or two actually said as much.

Only a couple of hours earlier, as I hurried in the opposite direction, there had been hardly anyone on this road. In places now, the crowds were as large and boisterous as in Ludhiana, maybe more. All out to see us, greet us, join in our slogans. Some even to walk with us—I remember a group of five or six teenage boys running up, mingling with us, walking along for a good fifteen minutes, laughing and waving. It was a slap in the face of all my fears about the Yatra in Kashmir. Nobody I saw looked even indifferent to our presence. Instead, they were smiling, shouting, waving, rushing up to shake hands.

It was exhilarating.

We made our way thus to Lal Chowk. By the time we reached, I had walked close to 20 km that day, a fair stretch of that at a cracking pace. But the adrenaline flowed so freely that I felt the weight of those kilometres hardly at all. Besides, there was all that was happening around me.

More assumptions busted, there in Lal Chowk. Far from just one flag being hastily raised under tight security—as earlier ideologues had reported and patted themselves on the back for—the whole plaza was awash in the tricolour. Yatris and locals mingled all over, chatting, taking selfies, raising slogans. The civil society group gathered below the famous clock tower and posed for photos in every possible permutation of themselves. Their very own flag-bearer—Virender, who had carried it all the way from Kanyakumari—stood there like a tree trunk, waving the flag this way and that.

* * *

Let's be clear: I have no illusions about the enormity of India's Kashmir tangle. I don't think anybody I met on the Yatra does either. We were and remain all too aware of the naysayers, whether in Kashmir or elsewhere in India. But for those exhilarating forty-five minutes in Lal Chowk, it was possible to drop the layers of wariness and scepticism. Possible to forget the hatreds. Possible to dream of something bigger and better. Possible to believe again in such words as brotherhood, friendship, understanding, freedom, hope, progress.

Peace.

That dream of peace. That was what the Yatra brought to Kashmir. To India.

7

Vision: What It All Means

Somewhere north of Sawai Madhopur, with dawn still to fully break, Ramani and I picked up some cold, delicious guavas from a local farmer. He had brought piles of them to the roadside for us walkers. Someone else on the Yatra had just told me about the famous guavas of this region, and now here was this man in a red turban, handing them out. At that moment, nothing could have tasted better. Fine start to the day.

Only a little further, still munching on my excellent guava, we saw some walkers ahead who had stopped for a few moments to marvel at a lone tree in a field to our right. It looked fairly nondescript. But when I got to where they were and took advantage of their angle of sight on the tree, I marvelled too: the rising sun, through its branches, was a striking image.

Having caught up with them, we walked together for a stretch. One of them was Avani, a lawyer from Delhi, educated at Oxford and Harvard. At a first quick glance, her white trousers and black sweater even made her look like a lawyer. She had taken an extended break from her legal work to join the Yatra. She had a lot to say about her experience, her expectations from the Yatra, the ways of the Congress Party. In particular, she hinted at diving into electoral politics from her home constituency of Harda in Madhya Pradesh.

I was intrigued by that mention of possibly standing for election but didn't get a chance to ask her to elaborate. Not even when we met again on the Punjab and Kashmir legs of the Yatra. So when, a few months after the end of the Yatra, I called to catch up with her, I was surprised and delighted to reach her in Harda. With Madhya Pradesh due to go to the polls late in 2023, she was there, about to plunge into an election campaign.

And it was going to be hard work. To begin with, she wasn't sure of getting a Congress ticket at all—to her knowledge, there were seven other contenders. The Harda seat is held by a man from the BJP, Kamal Patel, currently the state's Minister of Agriculture. He has won the seat five times since 1993, losing to the Congress only in 2013.

Beating him is a tall order. Besides, Avani is not from a political family and will have to learn the ropes, earn her political stripes, on the fly. Her successful legal practice in Delhi will take a hit, given that she will move to Harda for five or six months.

And yet, this is how she wants to do politics. Not as an appointed representative—the Rajya Sabha as opposed to the Lok Sabha, or the equivalent in the state—but stand and win. It promised to be raw, dirty, cut-throat—the attributes most of us believe apply to politics, that make most of us shy away from politics. Avani acknowledges those but thinks she has overcome her fears of them. That's the effect the Yatra has had on her, because of how it has introduced her to people of every stripe.

For a while between us, it was almost a meta-conversation. Maybe because Avani is new to this game, maybe because she dearly wants to find the approach that's right for her, maybe because she is less cynical and more idealistic about politics than many of her peers—whatever it is, she finds herself wrestling with questions about the nature of politics itself, about how she will fit the role. Not that this is unwelcome. On the contrary, to me, it seemed the Yatra had also made her eager for this introspection and reflection. Now she sees it as an intrinsic part of politics.

So I asked the question: what is politics to you, Avani?

That opened the floodgates. To begin with, she had started feeling superficial, 'internally dissatisfied', with what she was doing in Delhi. Eventually she knew: she needed to return to her roots, and for the long term. This informs the way she approaches the campaign. Every day, she finds herself asking, *Who am I working for?*

The question makes sense, because she has come to understand that as a politician, she has to become the voice of the people; a leader is someone who touches people's lives. And power, after all, lies in and with the people. So there were more questions to answer: *Have I done one good thing for the people of my city? Raised one important issue? Brought the people to the centre of my politics?* In a course on Constitutional Law when she was at Harvard, the professor, Richard Parker, challenged her on similar lines. 'If you're going to be a lawmaker,' he asked, 'why be afraid of people? Do you believe in the wisdom of the people? Or do you think you know what's best for them?'

Seek answers to all these, and an election ticket might come knocking.

Yet for all the worth of such questions, they remain intellectual exercises. How do they translate on the ground?

In the three months before our phone conversation, Avani had visited fifty villages in her constituency.

What that made clear to her is that battles in India are far more basic than the ones she would have had to fight had she stayed on in the UK or the US. 'There, it might be about equal pay for women,' she said. 'Here, it's about the right to the availability of work.'

One village in those fifty particularly stood out for her. This is a 'resettlement' village, for people whose original homes were submerged in the waters of the Narmada after dams were built on the river. The whole village is now on a hill, rising above the lake. When Avani visited, she was stunned to find the residents living 'like a thousand years ago'—with no school, no electricity. For work under the Indira Awas Yojana, they were told to return to their old homes further down the slope, visible in drier weather when the water level drops.

'They have nothing!' she said.

Soon after, she actually lived some of that herself, during a workshop she signed up for. This was a thirty-day exploration of political leadership, called Netrutva Sangam[8]. Sachin Rao, Training-in-Charge of the All-India Congress Committee, whom I had also seen on the Yatra, led the workshop.

Part of it was a stay in a remote village in Rajasthan; Avani's first experience living without electricity. Eight hundred homes there, without electricity. Yet just 400 metres beyond the last home is a newly built resort. Avani visited it, because she was on her period. It's a newly built resort supplied, naturally, with electricity. Yet only a few minutes' walk away, people live without. What are the lessons?

---

[8] https://sarvodayasangam.com/Web/netrutva-sangam-program (accessed November 10, 2023).

Rahul Gandhi spent a day at the same workshop. He brought them one word to discuss: *sadhana*. You could think it means learning, practice, maybe meditation. But maybe it suggests 'being in the flow'? No need to think of ends, or the path you're on; just finish your painting, don't worry about whether it will sell. Just be your whole self—head, heart and soul together—in whatever you're doing.

Are these spiritual, even metaphysical themes? Maybe so, but Avani's time on the Yatra prepped her for just such rumination. It taught her the meaning of having your feet on the ground, literally and figuratively. The vast variety of people who joined the Yatra, the conversations she had, the thoughts in her mind, the constant challenges to mind and body—these took it beyond the physical and made the Yatra a spiritual, emotional and intellectual journey, an experience like no other.

Curiously, the steady walking brought emotions bubbling up in ways she never expected. Once she was in tears all day. Another time, irritated for hours on end. Still another time, laughing. *Can I walk without thinking?* she'd wonder. In a profound sense, she found her emotions were all linked to her physical self, as she walked and walked even more, as 'my mind fell off', as she struggled to make sense of how she was still walking after all these months, after all these states.

'But these were all good things to happen,' she told me. She came to think of the Yatra as 'deep work'—as I understood it, the kind that makes great demands on you, but that touches you somewhere deep. Do deep work like that for five months, you lose all your failings.

As a testimonial to the Bharat Jodo Yatra, I'll take that.

* * *

Months after it ended, I look back at the Bharat Jodo Yatra in some wonder, and at two levels. First, that it happened at all, and actually stretched from Kanyakumari to Kashmir. Second, at what it did for me.

Before the Yatra began, I was a definite sceptic. I remember other such high-minded acts by politicians, after all. Sometime in 1993, for example, the then chief minister of Tamil Nadu, Jayalalitha, announced that she would go on a fast unto death over bringing Tamil Nadu what she often called its 'rightful share'[9] of the waters of

---

[9]   For example she once said this in the Tamil Nadu Assembly: 'I and my government are committed to securing the state's rightful share in the Cauvery waters.' See this report: https://economictimes.indiatimes.com/news/politics-and-nation/tamil-nadu-clears-it-would-not-allow-construction-of-new-dam-by-karnataka/articleshow/12468351.cms (accessed 5 October 2023).

the Cauvery River. Now the Cauvery's bounty has been shared by Karnataka and Tamil Nadu for decades, if with simmering resentments perennially ready to be stoked by politicians on both sides. Never mind that, though. The notion of the head of the state government, no less, fasting for something like this should itself have been a red flag. Perhaps it was, because I was—like before the Yatra—sceptical.

Jayalalitha proved my scepticism was largely justified. Her minions erected a stage on Chennai's Marina Beach, complete with a roof and fans and no doubt plenty of other comforts. She sat there for eighty hours, with a stream of partymen and friendly politicians stopping by to offer their support. Also doctors who would report gravely on her deteriorating health. When the Central Government gave her some kind of assurance, she pronounced success and called off the fast. I don't mean to turn up my nose at the eighty hours. But in comparison to other fasts by figures like M.K. Gandhi and Medha Patkar, I'll just say Jayalalitha's effort was some way short of persuasive.

I actually thought of Jayalalitha's fast before the Yatra started. Would my scepticism be similarly justified? Would Rahul Gandhi and his Congress colleagues walk a day or two, maybe a week or two, pronounce it a success and call it off?

Turns out they didn't do that. Turns out they walked for five months, all the way to Kashmir. At some level, it doesn't matter to me what long-term effect the Yatra will have, if any. Because this simple act of staying the course is itself a revelation. That grit and tenacity touch me somewhere deep, maybe because I never had it, but even more so because it persuades me that I can find it. Even though my time on the Yatra was almost vanishingly short compared to so many others, it still took plenty out of me, physically and mentally. But I wanted to do it. Partly, I wanted to test myself. But mostly, in these times and in this climate we're in, I wanted some way to stand up and be counted. Or maybe, that was a test too.

And yet, what of the long term? What of the future? After all, that was a much-discussed question among those I walked with. It was usually followed by plenty of speculation about a west-to-east Yatra, from Gujarat to Mizoram or Arunachal (not so much talk of east-to-west, though, except briefly when we walked with Rahul Gandhi). I don't know if the party is planning one such. If there is one, I will want to join it as well. Stand up and be counted, again.

And yet 'another Yatra' doesn't answer the questions. It will fill another five or six months, but then what? Still another Yatra? Clearly not. At some point, the party and the rest of us will have to reckon with what we think we're standing up and being counted for.

So for me, it goes like this. Just as much as I thought Indira Gandhi and her Emergency had to be defeated, all the way back in 1977, I think the BJP and its ideology must be defeated today. As a college student in 1977, I believed the very existence of a democratic India was in danger from the Emergency. As a greying 'veteran' journalist—I was first described that way over ten years ago—today, I believe democratic India is in danger again, but this time from the BJP. This is what needs ever more of us to stand up and be counted. To me, it's that simple.

* * *

The truth is, though, that the defeat of the BJP is almost secondary. Of course I joined the Yatra with that in mind, and assumed that everyone else in the Yatra had it in mind as well. And maybe we all did. But put it this way: the Yatra gave that goal some perspective. What matters to me, even more than defeating the BJP, is a return to a certain kind of politics; in fact, to a certain kind of society I think we once had. Where when we disagreed, we did it with respect. Where we listened, even when we disagreed. Where politicians paid attention to those who elected them, those they represented. Where we didn't immediately assume that someone with a different opinion was a fraud, or an enabler of terrorists, or a traitor, or unaffected by murder . . . I don't have to like that other person, you know, but I don't have to think the worst of her either.

Where we, in short, treated each other as just other humans.

After each of my four stints on the Yatra, I returned home with blistered feet and aching knees.

I expected that. What I didn't expect was a degree of mental fatigue as well. Understand, though, this wasn't in the least unwelcome. I knew this as the comedown after the intensity of the experience, the endless stimulation, as we walked. As much as I like my life, which I do, there's nothing in it quite like the sensory and emotional assault the Yatra offered. Every time, that feeling pushed me into thinking about my next visit: the where, the when, the how. Possibly even the why.

When the Yatra was over, of course, there was no next visit to look forward to. But I had inside me not just an overflow of memories, but a fistful of satisfaction, hope and optimism. All of which have been in short supply and eroded anyway, over several years now. Now, I can at least feel them.

This is why Avani's outlook on her election campaign struck such a chord. Again, of course her intent is to defeat the BJP incumbent in her constituency. But it's the way she